LOUISIANA CODE OF EVIDENCE 2020

About the Book

Formatted and compiled with the practitioners and law students in mind, this edition of the Louisiana Code of Evidence has easy to read text on letter size pages that reads across the whole page (no dual columns) and a detailed table of contents that allows you to quickly access the provision you need. Contains all articles as amended through the 2019 Regular Legislative Session. To browse online, visit www.CodeofEvidence.com.

About the Publisher

Access the law at your fingertips with Gulf Coast Legal Publishing, LLC. We're dedicated to providing legal professionals and law students with high quality, reasonably priced, user friendly legal titles. Founded by Nicholas M. Graphia, a practicing Louisiana lawyer frustrated with the limited options available for legal titles, many being overpriced, printed on small pages in small sized font, and filled with excessive editorial materials—Gulf Coast Legal Publishing's mission is deliver value for all readers.

For feedback and bulk order inquiries, email info@gulfcoastlegalpublishing.com.

Visit www.GulfCoastLegalPublishing.com to view recent legislative amendments and see our complete selection of Federal and Louisiana titles.

Copyright and ISBN

ISBN: 9781704022796

Contents

CHAPTER 1. GENERAL PROVISIONS

Art. 101. Scope

This Code governs proceedings in the courts of Louisiana to the extent and with the exceptions stated in Article 1101.
Acts 1988, No. 515, §1, eff. Jan. 1, 1989.

Art. 102. Purpose and construction

These articles shall be construed to secure fairness and efficiency in administration of the law of evidence to the end that the truth may be ascertained and proceedings justly determined.
Acts 1988, No. 515, §1, eff. Jan. 1, 1989.

Art. 103. Rulings on evidence

A. Effect of erroneous ruling. Error may not be predicated upon a ruling which admits or excludes evidence unless a substantial right of the party is affected, and

(1) Ruling admitting evidence. When the ruling is one admitting evidence, a timely objection or motion to admonish the jury to limit or disregard appears of record, stating the specific ground of objection; or

(2) Ruling excluding evidence. When the ruling is one excluding evidence, the substance of the evidence was made known to the court by counsel.

B. Record of ruling. The court may add any other or further statement which shows the character of the evidence, the form in which it was offered, the objection made, and the ruling thereon.

C. Hearing of jury. In jury cases, proceedings shall be conducted, to the extent practicable, so as to prevent inadmissible evidence from being suggested to the jury by any means, such as making statements or asking questions in the hearing of the jury.
Acts 1988, No. 515, §1, eff. Jan. 1, 1989.

Art. 104. Preliminary questions
NOTE: SEE C.E. ART. 1103.

A. Questions of admissibility generally. Preliminary questions concerning the competency or qualification of a person to be a witness, the existence of a privilege, or the admissibility of evidence shall be determined by the court, subject to the provisions of Paragraph B. In making its determination it is not bound by the rules of evidence except those with respect to privileges.

B. Relevancy conditioned on fact. Subject to other provisions of this Code, when the relevancy of evidence depends upon the fulfillment of a condition of fact, the court shall admit it upon, or subject to, the introduction of evidence sufficient to support a finding of the fulfillment of the condition.

C. Hearing of jury. Hearings on matters to be decided by the judge alone shall be conducted out of the hearing of the jury when the interests of justice require. Hearings on the admissibility of confessions or admissions by the accused or evidence allegedly unlawfully obtained shall in all cases be conducted out of the hearing of the jury, but when there has been a ruling prior to trial, it shall not be necessary to conduct another hearing as to admissibility before presentation of the evidence to a jury.

D. Weight and credibility. The preliminary determination by the court that evidence is admissible does not limit the right of a party to introduce evidence relevant to weight or credibility at the trial.

Acts 1988, No. 515, §1, eff. Jan. 1, 1989.

Art. 105. Limited admissibility

When evidence which is admissible as to one party or for one purpose but not admissible as to another party or for another purpose is admitted, the court, upon request, shall restrict the evidence to its proper scope and instruct the jury accordingly. Failure to restrict the evidence and instruct the jury shall not constitute error absent a request to do so.

Acts 1988, No. 515, §1, eff. Jan. 1, 1989.

CHAPTER 2. JUDICIAL NOTICE

Art. 201. Judicial notice of adjudicative facts generally

A. Scope of Article. This Article governs only judicial notice of adjudicative facts. An "adjudicative fact" is a fact normally determined by the trier of fact.

B. Kinds of facts. A judicially noticed fact must be one not subject to reasonable dispute in that it is either:

(1) Generally known within the territorial jurisdiction of the trial court; or

(2) Capable of accurate and ready determination by resort to sources whose accuracy cannot reasonably be questioned.

C. When discretionary. A court may take judicial notice, whether requested or not.

D. When mandatory. A court shall take judicial notice upon request if supplied with the information necessary for the court to determine that there is no reasonable dispute as to the fact.

E. Opportunity to be heard. A party is entitled upon timely request to an opportunity to be heard as to the propriety of taking judicial notice and the tenor of the matter noticed. In the absence of prior opportunity to be heard, the request may be made after judicial notice has been taken.

F. Time of taking notice. A party may request judicial notice at any stage of the proceeding but shall not do so in the hearing of a jury. Before taking judicial notice of a matter in its instructions to the jury, the court shall inform the parties before closing arguments begin.

G. Instructing jury. In a civil case, the court shall instruct the jury to accept as conclusive any fact judicially noticed. In a criminal case, the court shall instruct the jury that it may, but is not required to, accept as conclusive any fact judicially noticed.

Acts 1988, No. 515, §1, eff. Jan. 1, 1989.

Art. 202. Judicial notice of legal matters

A. Mandatory. A court, whether requested to do so or not, shall take judicial notice of the laws of the United States, of every state, territory, and other jurisdiction of the United States, and of the ordinances enacted by any political subdivision within the court's territorial jurisdiction whenever certified copies of the ordinances have been filed with the clerk of that court.

B. Other legal matters. (1) A court shall take judicial notice of the following if a party requests it and provides the court with the information needed by it to comply with the request, and may take judicial notice without request of a party of:

(a) Proclamations of the President of the United States and the governor of this state.

(b) Rules of boards, commissions, and agencies of this state that have been duly published and promulgated in the Louisiana Register.

(c) Ordinances enacted by any political subdivision of the State of Louisiana.

(d) Rules which govern the practice and procedure in a court of the United States or of any state, territory, or other jurisdiction of the United States, and which have been published in a form which makes them readily accessible.

(e) Rules and decisions of boards, commissions, and agencies of the United States or of any state, territory, or other jurisdiction of the United States which have been duly published and promulgated and which have the effect of law within their respective jurisdictions.

(f) Law of foreign countries, international law, and maritime law.

(2) A party who requests that judicial notice be taken and the court, if notice is taken without request shall give reasonable notice during trial to all other parties.

C. Information by court. The court may inform itself of any of the foregoing legal matters in such manner as it may deem proper, and the court may call upon counsel to aid it in obtaining such information.

D. Time of taking notice. Judicial notice of the foregoing legal matters may be taken at any stage of the proceeding, provided that before taking judicial notice of a matter in its instructions to the jury, the court shall inform the parties before closing arguments begin.

E. Question for court. The determination of the foregoing legal matters shall be made by the court.

Acts 1988, No. 515, §1, eff. Jan. 1, 1989.

CHAPTER 3. EFFECT IN CIVIL CASES OF

PRESUMPTIONS AND PRIMA FACIE EVIDENCE

Art. 301. Scope of Chapter

This Chapter applies only to civil cases. It defines and clarifies the foundation, weight, and other effects of presumptions and prima facie evidence or proof as used in legislation but does not apply where more specific legislation provides otherwise. It does not create new presumptions, nor does it apply to or directly affect mixed questions of law and fact, such as the inference of negligence arising from the doctrine of res ipsa loquitur.
Acts 1997, No. 577, §1.

Art. 302. Definitions

The following definitions apply under this Chapter:

(1) The "burden of persuasion" is the burden of a party to establish a requisite degree of belief in the mind of the trier of fact as to the existence or nonexistence of a fact. Depending on the circumstances, the degree of belief may be by a preponderance of the evidence, by clear and convincing evidence, or as otherwise required by law.

(2) A "predicate fact" is a fact or group of facts which must be established for a party to be entitled to the benefits of a presumption.

(3) A "presumption" is an inference created by legislation that the trier of fact must draw if it finds the existence of the predicate fact unless the trier of fact is persuaded by evidence of the nonexistence of the fact to be inferred. As used herein, it does not include a particular usage of the term "presumption" where the content, context, or history of the statute indicates an intention merely to authorize but not to require the trier of fact to draw an inference.

(4) An "inference" is a conclusion that an evidentiary fact exists based on the establishment of a predicate fact.
Acts 1997, No. 577, §1.

Art. 303. Conclusive presumptions

A "conclusive presumption" is a rule of substantive law and is not regulated by this Chapter.
Acts 1997, No. 577, §1.

Art. 304. Rebuttable presumptions

Presumptions regulated by this Chapter are rebuttable presumptions and therefore may be controverted or overcome by appropriate evidence.
Acts 1997, No. 577, §1.

Art. 305. Effect of presumptions if there is no controverting evidence

If the trier of fact finds the existence of the predicate fact, and there is no evidence controverting the fact to be inferred, the trier of fact is required to find the existence of the fact to be inferred.

Acts 1997, No. 577, §1.

Art. 306. Effect of presumptions if there is controverting evidence

If the trier of fact finds the existence of the predicate fact, and if there is evidence controverting the fact to be inferred, it shall find the existence of the inferred fact unless it is persuaded by the controverting evidence of the nonexistence of the inferred fact.

Acts 1997, No. 577, §1.

Art. 307. Jury instructions

In jury cases, upon request, the jury shall be instructed of the existence of a presumption and instructed as to its effect in accordance with Articles 305 and 306.

Acts 1997, No. 577, §1.

Art. 308. Effect of the term "prima facie" in legislation

A. Legislation providing that a document or other evidence is prima facie evidence or proof of all or part of its contents or of another fact establishes a presumption under this Chapter. When, however, the content, context, or history of the legislation indicates an intention not to shift the burden of persuasion, such legislation establishes only an inference and in a jury case, the court on request shall instruct the jury that if it finds the existence of the predicate fact it may but need not find the inferred fact.

B. Other uses of the term "prima facie", such as those that merely provide for the admissibility of specified evidence, do not create presumptions or inferences and are not regulated by this Chapter.

Acts 1997, No. 577, §1.

CHAPTER 4. RELEVANCY AND ITS LIMITS

Art. 401. Definition of "relevant evidence"

"Relevant evidence" means evidence having any tendency to make the existence of any fact that is of consequence to the determination of the action more probable or less probable than it would be without the evidence.
Acts 1988, No. 515, §1, eff. Jan. 1, 1989.

Art. 402. Relevant evidence generally admissible; irrelevant evidence inadmissible

All relevant evidence is admissible, except as otherwise provided by the Constitution of the United States, the Constitution of Louisiana, this Code of Evidence, or other legislation. Evidence which is not relevant is not admissible.
Acts 1988, No. 515, §1, eff. Jan. 1, 1989.

Art. 403. Exclusion of relevant evidence on grounds of prejudice, confusion, or waste of time

Although relevant, evidence may be excluded if its probative value is substantially outweighed by the danger of unfair prejudice, confusion of the issues, or misleading the jury, or by considerations of undue delay, or waste of time.
Acts 1988, No. 515, §1, eff. Jan. 1, 1989.

Art. 404. Character evidence generally not admissible in civil or criminal trial to prove conduct; exceptions; other criminal acts

A. Character evidence generally. Evidence of a person's character or a trait of his character, such as a moral quality, is not admissible in a civil or criminal proceeding for the purpose of proving that he acted in conformity therewith on a particular occasion, except:

(1) Character of accused. Evidence of a pertinent trait of his character, such as a moral quality, offered by an accused, or by the prosecution to rebut the character evidence; provided that such evidence shall be restricted to showing those moral qualities pertinent to the crime with which he is charged, and that character evidence cannot destroy conclusive evidence of guilt.

(2) Character of victim. (a) Except as provided in Article 412, evidence of a pertinent trait of character, such as a moral quality, of the victim of the crime offered by an accused, or by the prosecution to rebut the character evidence; provided that in the absence of evidence of a hostile demonstration or an overt act on the part of the victim at the time of the offense charged, evidence of his dangerous character is not admissible; provided further that when the accused pleads self-defense and there is a history of assaultive behavior between the victim and the accused and the accused lived in a familial or intimate relationship such as, but not limited to, the husband-wife, parent-child, or concubinage relationship, it shall not be necessary to first show a hostile demonstration or overt act on the part of the victim in order to introduce evidence of the dangerous character of the victim, including specific instances of conduct and domestic violence; and further

13

provided that an expert's opinion as to the effects of the prior assaultive acts on the accused's state of mind is admissible; or

(b) Evidence of a character trait of peacefulness of the victim offered by the prosecution in a homicide case to rebut evidence that the victim was the first aggressor;

(3) Character of witness. Evidence of the character of a witness, as provided in Articles 607, 608, and 609.

B. Other crimes, wrongs, or acts. (1) Except as provided in Article 412, evidence of other crimes, wrongs, or acts is not admissible to prove the character of a person in order to show that he acted in conformity therewith. It may, however, be admissible for other purposes, such as proof of motive, opportunity, intent, preparation, plan, knowledge, identity, absence of mistake or accident, provided that upon request by the accused, the prosecution in a criminal case shall provide reasonable notice in advance of trial, of the nature of any such evidence it intends to introduce at trial for such purposes, or when it relates to conduct that constitutes an integral part of the act or transaction that is the subject of the present proceeding.

(2) In the absence of evidence of a hostile demonstration or an overt act on the part of the victim at the time of the offense charged, evidence of the victim's prior threats against the accused or the accused's state of mind as to the victim's dangerous character is not admissible; provided that when the accused pleads self-defense and there is a history of assaultive behavior between the victim and the accused and the accused lived in a familial or intimate relationship such as, but not limited to, the husband-wife, parent-child, or concubinage relationship, it shall not be necessary to first show a hostile demonstration or overt act on the part of the victim in order to introduce evidence of the dangerous character of the victim, including specific instances of conduct and domestic violence; and further provided that an expert's opinion as to the effects of the prior assaultive acts on the accused's state of mind is admissible.

Acts 1988, No. 515, §1, eff. Jan. 1, 1989; Acts 1994, 3rd Ex. Sess., No. 51, §1; Acts 2016, No. 357, §1.

Art. 405. Methods of proving character

A. Reputation. Except as provided in Article 412, in all cases in which evidence of character or a trait of character of a person is admissible, proof may be made by testimony as to general reputation only. On cross-examination of the character witness, inquiry is allowable into relevant specific instances of conduct.

B. Specific instances of conduct. In cases in which character or a trait of character of a person is an essential element of a charge, claim, or defense, such as in a prosecution for defamation or when there is a defense of entrapment, proof may also be made of specific instances of his conduct.

C. Foundation. Before a person may be permitted to testify to the reputation of another person, a foundation must be established that the witness is familiar with that reputation.

Acts 1988, No. 515, §1, eff. Jan. 1, 1989.

Art. 406. Habit; routine practice; methods of proof

Evidence of the habit of a person or of the routine practice of an organization, whether corroborated or not and regardless of the presence of eyewitnesses, is relevant to prove that the conduct of the person or organization on a particular occasion was in conformity with the habit or

routine practice. The evidence may consist of testimony in the form of an opinion or evidence of specific instances of conduct sufficient in number to warrant a finding that the habit existed or that the practice was routine.
Acts 1988, No. 515, §1, eff. Jan. 1, 1989.

Art. 407. Subsequent remedial measures

In a civil case, when, after an event, measures are taken which, if taken previously, would have made the event less likely to occur, evidence of the subsequent measures is not admissible to prove negligence or culpable conduct in connection with the event. This Article does not require the exclusion of evidence of subsequent measures when offered for another purpose, such as proving ownership, authority, knowledge, control, or feasibility of precautionary measures, or for attacking credibility.
Acts 1988, No. 515, §1, eff. Jan. 1, 1989.

Art. 408. Compromise and offers to compromise

A. Civil cases. In a civil case, evidence of (1) furnishing or offering or promising to furnish, or (2) accepting or offering or promising to accept, anything of value in compromising or attempting to compromise a claim which was disputed as to either validity or amount, is not admissible to prove liability for or invalidity of the claim or its amount. Evidence of conduct or statements made in compromise negotiations is likewise not admissible. This Article does not require the exclusion of any evidence otherwise admissible merely because it is presented in the course of compromise negotiations. This Article also does not require exclusion when the evidence is offered for another purpose, such as proving bias or prejudice of a witness, negativing a contention of undue delay, or proving an effort to obstruct a criminal investigation or prosecution.

B. Criminal cases. This Article does not require the exclusion in a criminal case of evidence of the actions or statements described in Paragraph A, above, or of a giving or offer to give anything of value by the accused in direct or indirect restitution to a victim.
Acts 1988, No. 515, §1, eff. Jan. 1, 1989.

Art. 409. Payment of medical and similar expenses

In a civil case, evidence of furnishing or offering or promising to pay expenses or losses occasioned by an injury to person or damage to property is not admissible to prove liability for the injury or damage nor is it admissible to mitigate, reduce, or avoid liability therefor. This Article does not require the exclusion of such evidence when it is offered solely for another purpose, such as to enforce a contract for payment.
Acts 1988, No. 515, §1, eff. Jan. 1, 1989.

Art. 410. Inadmissibility of pleas, plea discussions, and related statements

A. General rule. Except as otherwise provided in this Article, evidence of the following is not, in any civil or criminal proceeding, admissible against the party who made the plea or was a participant in the plea discussions:

(1) A plea of guilty or of nolo contendere which was later withdrawn or set aside;

(2) In a civil case, a plea of nolo contendere;

(3) Any statement made in the course of any court proceeding concerning either of the foregoing pleas, or any plea discussions with an attorney for or other representative of the prosecuting authority regarding either of the foregoing pleas; or

(4) Any statement made in the course of plea discussions with an attorney for or other representative of the prosecuting authority which do not result in a plea of guilty or which result in a plea of guilty later withdrawn or set aside.

B. Exceptions. However, such a statement is admissible:

(1) In any proceeding wherein another statement made in the course of the same plea or plea discussions has been introduced and the statement ought in fairness be considered contemporaneously with it; or

(2) In a criminal proceeding for perjury or false statement if the statement was made by the defendant under oath, on the record and in the presence of counsel.
Acts 1988, No. 515, §1, eff. Jan. 1, 1989.

Art. 411. Liability insurance

Although a policy of insurance may be admissible, the amount of coverage under the policy shall not be communicated to the jury unless the amount of coverage is a disputed issue which the jury will decide.
Acts 1988, No. 515, §1, eff. Jan. 1, 1989.

Art. 412. Victim's past sexual behavior in sexual assault cases; trafficking offenses

A.(1) Opinion and reputation evidence; sexual assault cases. When an accused is charged with a crime involving sexually assaultive behavior, reputation or opinion evidence of the past sexual behavior of the victim is not admissible.

(2) Other evidence; exceptions. When an accused is charged with a crime involving sexually assaultive behavior, evidence of specific instances of the victim's past sexual behavior is also not admissible except for:

(a) Evidence of past sexual behavior with persons other than the accused, upon the issue of whether or not the accused was the source of semen or injury; provided that such evidence is limited to a period not to exceed seventy-two hours prior to the time of the offense, and further provided that the jury be instructed at the time and in its final charge regarding the limited purpose for which the evidence is admitted; or

(b) Evidence of past sexual behavior with the accused offered by the accused upon the issue of whether or not the victim consented to the sexually assaultive behavior.

B.(1) Opinion and reputation evidence; trafficking. When an accused is charged with a crime involving human trafficking or trafficking of children for sexual purposes, reputation or opinion evidence of the past sexual behavior of the victim is not admissible.

(2) Evidence of specific instances of the victim's past sexual behavior is not admissible unless the evidence is offered by the prosecution in a criminal case to prove a pattern of trafficking activity by the defendant.

C. Motion. (1) Before the person, accused of committing a crime that involves sexually assaultive behavior, human trafficking, or trafficking of children for sexual purposes, may offer under Subparagraph (A)(2) or (B)(2) of this Article evidence of specific instances of the victim's past sexual behavior, the accused shall make a written motion in camera to offer such evidence. The motion shall be accompanied by a written statement of evidence setting forth the names and addresses of persons to be called as witnesses.

(2) The motion and statement of evidence shall be served on the state which shall make a reasonable effort to notify the victim prior to the hearing.

D. Time for a motion. The motion shall be made within the time for filing pre-trial motions specified in Code of Criminal Procedure Article 521, except that the court shall allow the motion to be made at a later date, if the court determines that:

(1) The evidence is of past sexual behavior with the accused, and the accused establishes that the motion was not timely made because of an impossibility arising through no fault of his own; or

(2) The evidence is of past sexual behavior with someone other than the accused, and the accused establishes that the evidence or the issue to which it relates is newly discovered and could not have been obtained earlier through the exercise of due diligence.

E. Hearing. (1) If the court determines that the statement of evidence contains evidence described in Subparagraph (A)(2) or (B)(2), the court shall order a hearing which shall be closed to determine if such evidence is admissible. At such hearing the parties may call witnesses.

(2) The victim, if present, has the right to attend the hearing and may be accompanied by counsel.

(3) If the court determines on the basis of the hearing described in Subparagraph (E)(1) that the evidence which the accused seeks to offer is relevant and that the probative value of such evidence outweighs the danger of unfair prejudice, such evidence may be admissible in the trial to the extent an order made by the court specifies evidence which may be offered and areas with respect to which the victim may be examined or cross-examined. Introduction of such evidence shall be limited to that specified in the order.

(4) Any motion made under Subparagraph C and any statement of evidence, brief, record of a hearing, or like material made or used in connection with the motion shall be kept in a separate, sealed package as part of the record in the case. Nothing in this Article shall preclude the use of the testimony at such hearing in a subsequent prosecution for perjury or false swearing.

F. Past sexual behavior defined. For purposes of this Article, the term "past sexual behavior" means sexual behavior other than the sexual behavior with respect to which the offense of sexually assaultive behavior is alleged.

G. The rules of admissibility of evidence provided by this Article shall also apply to civil actions brought by the victim which are alleged to arise from sexually assaultive behavior, human trafficking, or trafficking of children for sexual purposes by the defendant, whether or not convicted of such crimes.

Acts 1988, No. 515, §1, eff. Jan. 1, 1989; Acts 2014, No. 564, §5; Acts 2016, No. 357, §1.

Art. 412.1. Victim's attire in sexual assault cases

A. When an accused is charged with the crime of aggravated or first degree rape, forcible or second degree rape, simple or third degree rape, sexual battery, or second degree sexual battery, the manner and style of the victim's attire shall not be admissible as evidence that the victim encouraged or consented to the offense; however, items of clothing or parts thereof may be introduced in order to establish the presence or absence of the elements of the offense and the proof of its occurrence.

B. The rules of admissibility of evidence provided by this Article shall also apply to civil actions brought by the victim which are alleged to arise from the crimes of aggravated or first degree rape, forcible or second degree rape, simple or third degree rape, sexual battery, or second degree sexual battery committed by the defendant, whether or not convicted of such crimes.
Acts 1992, No. 725, §1; Acts 2004, No. 676, §4; Acts 2015, No. 184, §7; Acts 2016, No. 357, §1.

Art. 412.2. Evidence of similar crimes, wrongs, or acts in sex offense cases

A. When an accused is charged with a crime involving sexually assaultive behavior, or with acts that constitute a sex offense involving a victim who was under the age of seventeen at the time of the offense, evidence of the accused's commission of another crime, wrong, or act involving sexually assaultive behavior or acts which indicate a lustful disposition toward children may be admissible and may be considered for its bearing on any matter to which it is relevant subject to the balancing test provided in Article 403.

B. In a case in which the state intends to offer evidence under the provisions of this Article, the prosecution shall, upon request of the accused, provide reasonable notice in advance of trial of the nature of any such evidence it intends to introduce at trial for such purposes.

C. This Article shall not be construed to limit the admission or consideration of evidence under any other rule.
Acts 2001, No. 1130, §1; Acts 2004, No. 465, §1.

Art. 412.3. Statements made by victims of trafficking during investigations

If a victim of human trafficking or trafficking of children for sexual purposes is also a defendant in any case arising from unlawful acts committed as part of the same trafficking activity, any inculpatory statement made by the victim as a result of questioning by any person then known by the victim to be a law enforcement officer is inadmissible against the victim, except pursuant to Article 801 of this Code or in any prosecution of the victim for perjury, at a trial of the victim for the unlawful acts committed by the victim as part of the same trafficking activity if all of the following conditions exist:

(1) The victim cooperates with the investigation and prosecution, including the giving of a use-immunity statement as directed by the prosecuting attorney.

(2) The victim testifies truthfully at any hearing or trial related to the trafficking activity, or agrees, either in writing or on the record, to testify truthfully at any hearing or trial related to the trafficking activity in any prosecution of any other person charged with an offense arising from the same trafficking activity, regardless of whether the testimony is unnecessary due to entry of a plea by the other person.

(3) The victim has agreed in writing to receive services or participate in a program that provides services to victims of human trafficking or trafficking of children for sexual purposes, if such services are available.
Acts 2014, No. 564, §5.

Art. 412.4. Evidence of similar crimes, wrongs, or acts in domestic abuse cases and cruelty against juveniles cases

A. When an accused is charged with a crime involving abusive behavior against a family member, household member, or dating partner or with acts which constitute cruelty involving a victim who was under the age of seventeen at the time of the offense, evidence of the accused's commission of another crime, wrong, or act involving assaultive behavior against a family member, household member, or dating partner or acts which constitute cruelty involving a victim who was under the age of seventeen at the time of the offense, may be admissible and may be considered for its bearing on any matter to which it is relevant, subject to the balancing test provided in Article 403.

B. In a case in which the state intends to offer evidence under the provisions of this Article, the prosecution shall, upon request of the accused, provide reasonable notice in advance of trial of the nature of any such evidence it intends to introduce at trial for such purposes.

C. This Article shall not be construed to limit the admissibility or consideration of evidence under any other rule.

D. For purposes of this Article:

(1) "Abusive behavior" means any behavior of the offender involving the use or threatened use of force against the person or property of a family member, household member, or dating partner of the alleged offender.

(2) "Dating partner" means any person who is involved or has been involved in a sexual or intimate relationship with the offender characterized by the expectation of affectionate involvement independent of financial considerations, regardless of whether the person presently lives or formerly lived in the same residence with the offender. "Dating partner" shall not include a casual relationship or ordinary association between persons in a business or social context.

(3) "Family member" means spouses, former spouses, parents and children, stepparents, stepchildren, foster parents, and foster children.

(4) "Household member" means any person having reached the age of majority presently or formerly living in the same residence with the offender as a spouse, whether married or not, or any child presently or formerly living in the same residence with the offender, or any child of the offender regardless of where the child resides.

Acts 2016, No. 399, §1; Acts 2017, No. 84, §4.

Art. 412.5. Evidence of similar crimes, wrongs, or acts in certain civil cases

A. In any civil action alleging acts of domestic abuse as defined in R.S. 46:2132, family violence as defined in R.S. 9:362, or sexual abuse as defined in R.S. 9:362, evidence of the defendant's commission of a crime, wrong, or act involving acts of domestic abuse, family violence, or sexual abuse may be admissible and may be considered for its bearing on any matter to which it is relevant subject to the balancing test provided in Article 403.

B. A plaintiff in a tort action intending to offer evidence under the provisions of this Article shall provide reasonable notice in advance of trial of the nature of such evidence.

C. The provisions of this Article shall not be construed to preclude or limit the introduction or consideration of any evidence otherwise authorized under law.

Acts 2018, No. 228, §1, eff. May 15, 2018.

Art. 413. Settlement or tender

Any amount paid in settlement or by tender shall not be admitted into evidence unless the failure to make a settlement or tender is an issue in the case.
Acts 1988, No. 515, §1, eff. Jan. 1, 1989.

Art. 414. Worker's compensation payments

Evidence of the nature and extent of a worker's compensation claim or of payment of past or future worker's compensation benefits shall not be admissible to a jury, directly or indirectly, in any civil proceeding with respect to a claim for damages relative to the same injury for which the worker's compensation benefits are claimed or paid. Such evidence shall be admissible and presented to the judge only.
Acts 1990, No. 973, §2.

Art. 415. Act of contacting or retaining an attorney

In any criminal proceeding, the act of contacting or retaining an attorney shall not be admissible against any individual or entity, unless such act falls within an established exception for crime or fraud.
Acts 1993, No. 626, §1.

CHAPTER 5. TESTIMONIAL PRIVILEGES

Art. 501. Scope of privileges

Privileges as recognized in this Chapter are evidentiary in nature, do not of themselves create causes of action or other substantive rights, and are applicable to proceedings enumerated in Article 1101. Nothing in this Chapter is intended to regulate the content or waiver of constitutional rights, nor inferences to be drawn from their invocation.
Acts 1992, No. 376, §1, eff. Jan. 1, 1993.

Art. 502. Waiver of privilege

A. Waiver. A person upon whom the law confers a privilege against disclosure waives the privilege if he or his predecessor while holder of the privilege voluntarily discloses or consents to disclosure of any significant part of the privileged matter. This rule does not apply if the disclosure itself is privileged.

B. Disclosure under compulsion or without opportunity to claim. A claim of privilege is not defeated by a disclosure which was compelled or made without opportunity to claim the privilege.

C. Joint holders. Where two or more persons are joint holders of a privilege, a waiver of the right of one joint holder to claim the privilege does not affect the right of another joint holder to claim the privilege.
Acts 1992, No. 376, §1, eff. Jan. 1, 1993.

Art. 503. Comment on or inference from claim of privilege; instructions; exception

A. Comment, inference, and instructions.

(1) The claim of privilege, whether in the present proceeding or upon a prior occasion, is not a proper subject of comment by judge or counsel. No inferences may be drawn therefrom.

(2) In jury cases, proceedings shall be conducted, to the extent practicable, so as to facilitate the making of claims of privilege without the knowledge of the jury.

(3) Upon request, any party against whom the jury might draw an adverse inference from a claim of privilege is entitled to an instruction that no inference may be drawn therefrom.

B. Exception in non-criminal proceedings. In non-criminal proceedings, under exceptional circumstances in the interest of justice, if a claim of privilege is sustained counsel may comment thereon, and, upon request, the court shall instruct the trier of fact that it may draw all reasonable inferences therefrom.
Acts 1992, No. 376, §1, eff. Jan. 1, 1993.

Art. 504. Spousal confidential communications privilege

A. Definition. A communication is "confidential" if it is made privately and is not intended for further disclosure unless such disclosure is itself privileged.

B. Confidential communications privilege. Each spouse has a privilege during and after the marriage to refuse to disclose, and to prevent the other spouse from disclosing, confidential communications with the other spouse while they were husband and wife.

C. Confidential communications; exceptions. This privilege does not apply:

(1) In a criminal case in which one spouse is charged with a crime against the person or property of the other spouse or of a child of either.

(2) In a civil case brought by or on behalf of one spouse against the other spouse.

(3) In commitment or interdiction proceedings as to either spouse.

(4) When the communication is offered to protect or vindicate the rights of a minor child of either spouse.

(5) In cases otherwise provided by legislation.

Acts 1992, No. 376, §1, eff. Jan. 1, 1993.

Art. 505. Spousal witness privilege

In a criminal case or in commitment or interdiction proceedings, a witness spouse has a privilege not to testify against the other spouse. This privilege terminates upon the annulment of the marriage, legal separation, or divorce of the spouses. This privilege does not apply in a criminal case in which one spouse is charged with a crime against the person of the other spouse or a crime against the person of a child including but not limited to the violation of a preliminary or permanent injunction or protective order and violations of R.S. 14:79.

Acts 1992, No. 376, §1, eff. Jan. 1, 1993; Acts 2006, No. 191, §1.

Art. 506. Lawyer-client privilege

A. Definitions. As used in this Article:

(1) "Client" is a person, including a public officer, corporation, partnership, unincorporated association, or other organization or entity, public or private, to whom professional legal services are rendered by a lawyer, or who consults a lawyer with a view to obtaining professional legal services from the lawyer.

(2) "Representative of the client" is:

(a) A person having authority to obtain professional legal services, or to act on advice so obtained, on behalf of the client.

(b) Any other person who makes or receives a confidential communication for the purpose of effectuating legal representation for the client, while acting in the scope of employment for the client.

(3) "Lawyer" is a person authorized, or reasonably believed by the client to be authorized, to practice law in any state or nation.

(4) "Representative of the lawyer" is a person engaged by the lawyer to assist the lawyer in the lawyer's rendition of professional legal services.

(5) A communication is "confidential" if it is not intended to be disclosed to persons other than:

(a) Those to whom disclosure is made in furtherance of obtaining or rendering professional legal services for the client.

(b) Those reasonably necessary for the transmission of the communication.

(c) When special circumstances warrant, those who are present at the behest of the client and are reasonably necessary to facilitate the communication.

B. General rule of privilege. A client has a privilege to refuse to disclose, and to prevent another person from disclosing, a confidential communication, whether oral, written, or otherwise, made for the purpose of facilitating the rendition of professional legal services to the client, as well as the perceptions, observations, and the like, of the mental, emotional, or physical condition of the client in connection with such a communication, when the communication is:

(1) Between the client or a representative of the client and the client's lawyer or a representative of the lawyer.

(2) Between the lawyer and a representative of the lawyer.

(3) By the client or his lawyer, or a representative of either, to a lawyer, or representative of a lawyer, who represents another party concerning a matter of common interest.

(4) Between representatives of the client or between the client and a representative of the client.

(5) Among lawyers and their representatives representing the same client.

(6) Between representatives of the client's lawyer.

C. Exceptions. There is no privilege under this Article as to a communication:

(1)(a) If the services of the lawyer were sought or obtained to enable or aid anyone to commit or plan to commit what the client or his representative knew or reasonably should have known to be a crime or fraud.

(b) Made in furtherance of a crime or fraud.

(2) Which was with a client now deceased relevant to an issue between parties who claim through that client, regardless of whether the claims are by testate or intestate succession or by transaction inter vivos.

(3) Which is relevant to an issue of breach of duty by a lawyer to the client or by a client to the client's lawyer.

(4)(a) Which is relevant to an issue of authenticity or capacity concerning a document which the lawyer signed as a witness or notary.

(b) Concerning the testimony of a representative of a lawyer regarding a communication relevant to an issue of authenticity or capacity concerning a document to which the representative is a witness or notary.

(5) Which is relevant to a matter of common interest between or among two or more clients if the communication was made by any of them or their representative to a lawyer or his representative retained or consulted in common, when subsequently offered by one client against the other in a civil action.

(6) Concerning the identity of the lawyer's client or his representative, unless disclosure of the identity by the lawyer or his representative would reveal either the reason for which legal services were sought or a communication which is otherwise privileged under this Article.

D. Who may claim privilege. The privilege may be claimed by the client, the client's agent or legal representative, or the successor, trustee, or similar representative of a client that is a corporation, partnership, unincorporated association, or other organization, whether or not in existence. The person who was the lawyer or the lawyer's representative at the time of the communication is presumed to have authority to claim the privilege on behalf of the client, former client, or deceased client.

Acts 1992, No. 376, §1, eff. Jan. 1, 1993.

Art. 507. Subpoena of lawyer or his representative in criminal cases

A. General rule. Neither a subpoena nor a court order shall be issued to a lawyer or his representative to appear or testify in any criminal investigation or proceeding where the purpose of the subpoena or order is to ask the lawyer or his representative to reveal information about a client or former client obtained in the course of representing the client unless the court after a contradictory hearing has determined that the information sought is not protected from disclosure by any applicable privilege or work product rule; and all of the following:

(1) The information sought is essential to the successful completion of an ongoing investigation, prosecution, or defense.

(2) The purpose of seeking the information is not to harass the attorney or his client.

(3) With respect to a subpoena, the subpoena lists the information sought with particularity, is reasonably limited as to subject matter and period of time, and gives timely notice.

(4) There is no practicable alternative means of obtaining the information.

B. Waiver. Failure to object timely to non-compliance with the terms of this Article constitutes a waiver of the procedural protections of this Article, but does not constitute a waiver of any privilege.

C. Binding effect of determination; notice to client. The determination that a lawyer-client privilege is not applicable to the testimony shall not bind the client or former client unless the client or former client was given notice of the time, place, and substance of the hearing and had an opportunity fully to participate in that hearing.

D. Exceptions. This Article shall not apply in habitual offender proceedings when a lawyer is called as a witness for purposes of identification of his client or former client, or in post-conviction proceedings when a lawyer is called as a witness on the issue of ineffective assistance of the lawyer.

E. The procedural provisions and protections afforded by Paragraph A of this Article shall extend to lawyers serving as prosecutors in state, parish, or municipal courts, whether those functions are exercised in the name of the state of Louisiana or any parish or municipality, and whether the lawyer is the attorney general or assistant attorney general, a district attorney or assistant district attorney, or a parish or municipal prosecutor, and shall extend to lawyers employed by either house of the Louisiana Legislature.

Acts 1992, No. 376, §1, eff. Jan. 1, 1993; Acts 2007, No. 23, §1.

Art. 508. Subpoena of lawyer or his representative in civil cases

A. General rule. Neither a subpoena nor a court order shall be issued to a lawyer or his representative to appear or testify in any civil or juvenile proceeding, including pretrial discovery, or in an administrative investigation or hearing, where the purpose of the subpoena or order is to ask the lawyer or his representative to reveal information about a client or former client obtained in the course of representing the client unless, after a contradictory hearing, it has been determined that the information sought is not protected from disclosure by any applicable privilege or work product rule; and all of the following:

(1) The information sought is essential to the successful completion of an ongoing investigation, is essential to the case of the party seeking the information, and is not merely peripheral, cumulative, or speculative.

(2) The purpose of seeking the information is not to harass the attorney or his client.

(3) With respect to a subpoena, the subpoena lists the information sought with particularity, is reasonably limited as to subject matter and period of time, and gives timely notice.

(4) There is no practicable alternative means of obtaining the information.

B. Waiver. Failure to object timely to non-compliance with the terms of this Article constitutes a waiver of the procedural protections of this Article, but does not constitute a waiver of any privilege.

C. Binding effect of determination; notice to client. The determination that a lawyer-client privilege is not applicable to the testimony shall not bind the client or former client unless the client or former client was given notice of the time, place, and substance of the hearing and had an opportunity fully to participate in that hearing.

D. Scope. Nothing in this Article is intended to affect the provisions of Code of Civil Procedure Articles 863 and 1452(B).

E. The procedural provisions and protections afforded by Paragraph A of this Article shall extend to lawyers representing the state or any political subdivision, whether the lawyer is the attorney general or assistant attorney general, a district attorney or assistant district attorney, a parish attorney or assistant parish attorney; or a municipal or city attorney or assistant municipal or assistant city attorney; and shall extend to lawyers employed by either house of the Louisiana Legislature.

Acts 1992, No. 376, §1, eff. Jan. 1, 1993; Acts 2007, No. 23, §1.

Art. 509. Work product rule not affected

Nothing in this Chapter shall be construed as derogating from the protection afforded by the rules relating to work product.

Acts 1992, No. 376, §1, eff. Jan. 1, 1993.

Art. 510. Health care provider-patient privilege

A. Definitions. (1) The definitions of health care provider, physician, psychotherapist, and their representatives as provided in this Article include persons reasonably believed to be such by the patient or his representative. As used in this Article:

(1)(a) "Confidential communication" is the transmittal or acquisition of information not intended to be disclosed to persons other than:

(i) A health care provider and a representative of a health care provider.

(ii) Those reasonably necessary for the transmission of the communication.

(iii) Persons who are participating in the diagnosis and treatment under the direction of the physician or psychotherapist.

(iv) A patient's health care insurer, including any entity that provides indemnification to a patient.

(v) When special circumstances warrant, those who are present at the behest of the patient, physician, or psychotherapist and are reasonably necessary to facilitate the communication.

(b) "Confidential communication" includes any information, substance, or tangible object, obtained incidental to the communication process and any opinion formed as a result of the consultation, examination, or interview and also includes medical and hospital records made by health care providers and their representatives.

(2) "Health care provider" is a person or entity defined as such in R.S. 13:3734(A)(1), and includes a physician and psychotherapist as defined below, and also includes a person who is engaged in any office, center, or institution referred to as a rape crisis center, who has undergone at least forty hours of sexual assault training and who is engaged in rendering advice, counseling, or assistance to victims of sexual assault.

(3) "Health condition" is a physical, mental, or emotional condition, including a condition induced by alcohol, drugs, or other substance.

(4) "Patient" is a person who consults or is examined or interviewed by another for the purpose of receiving advice, diagnosis, or treatment in regard to that person's health.

(5) "Physician" is a person licensed to practice medicine in any state or nation.

(6) "Psychotherapist" is:

(a) A physician engaged in the diagnosis or treatment of a mental or emotional condition, including a condition induced by alcohol, drugs, or other substance.

(b) A person licensed or certified as a psychologist under the laws of any state or nation.

(c) A person licensed as a licensed professional counselor or social worker under the laws of any state or nation.

(7) "Representative" of a physician, psychotherapist, or other health care provider is:

(a) A person acting under the supervision, direction, control, or request of a physician, psychotherapist, or health care provider engaged in the diagnosis or treatment of the patient.

(b) Personnel of a "hospital", as defined in R.S. 13:3734(A)(3), whose duties relate to the health care of patients or to maintenance of patient records.

(8) "Representative of a patient" is any person who makes or receives a confidential communication for the purpose of effectuating diagnosis or treatment of a patient.

B.(1) General rule of privilege in civil proceedings. In a non-criminal proceeding, a patient has a privilege to refuse to disclose and to prevent another person from disclosing a confidential communication made for the purpose of advice, diagnosis or treatment of his health condition between or among himself or his representative, his health care provider, or their representatives.

(2) Exceptions. There is no privilege under this Article in a noncriminal proceeding as to a communication:

(a) When the communication relates to the health condition of a patient who brings or asserts a personal injury claim in a judicial or worker's compensation proceeding.

(b) When the communication relates to the health condition of a deceased patient in a wrongful death, survivorship, or worker's compensation proceeding brought or asserted as a consequence of the death or injury of the deceased patient.

(c) When the communication is relevant to an issue of the health condition of the patient in any proceeding in which the patient is a party and relies upon the condition as an element of his claim or defense or, after the patient's death, in any proceeding in which a party deriving his right from the patient relies on the patient's health condition as an element of his claim or defense.

(d) When the communication relates to the health condition of a patient when the patient is a party to a proceeding for custody or visitation of a child and the condition has a substantial bearing on the fitness of the person claiming custody or visitation, or when the patient is a child who is the subject of a custody or visitation proceeding.

(e) When the communication made to the health care provider was intended to assist the patient or another person to commit or plan to commit what the patient knew or reasonably should have known to be a crime or fraud.

(f) When the communication is made in the course of an examination ordered by the court with respect to the health condition of a patient, the fact that the examination was so ordered was made known to the patient prior to the communication, and the communication concerns the particular purpose for which the examination was made, unless the court in its order directing the examination has stated otherwise.

(g)(i) When the communication is made by a patient who is the subject of an interdiction or commitment proceeding to his current health care provider when such patient has failed or refused to submit to an examination by a health care provider appointed by the court regarding issues relating to the interdiction or commitment proceeding, provided that the patient has been advised of such appointment and the consequences of not submitting to the examination.

(ii) Notwithstanding the provisions of Subitem (i) of this Item, in any commitment proceeding, the court-appointed physician may review the medical records of the patient or respondent and testify as to communications therein, but only those which are essential to determine whether the patient is dangerous to himself, dangerous to others, or unable to survive safely in freedom or protect himself from serious harm. However, such communications shall not be disclosed unless the patient was informed prior to the communication that such communications are not privileged in any subsequent commitment proceedings. The court-appointed examination shall be governed by Item B(2)(f).

(h) When the communication is relevant in proceedings held by peer review committees and other disciplinary bodies to determine whether a particular health care provider has deviated from applicable professional standards.

(i) When the communication is one regarding the blood alcohol level or other test for the presence of drugs of a patient and an action for damages for injury, death, or loss has been brought against the patient.

(j) When disclosure of the communication is necessary for the defense of the health care provider in a malpractice action brought by the patient.

(k) When the communication is relevant to proceedings concerning issues of child abuse, elder abuse, or the abuse of persons with disabilities or persons who are incompetent.

(l) When the communication is relevant after the death of a patient, concerning the capacity of the patient to enter into the contract which is the subject matter of the litigation.

(m) When the communication is relevant in an action contesting any testament executed or claimed to have been executed by the patient now deceased.

C.(1) General rule of privilege in criminal proceedings. In a criminal proceeding, a patient has a privilege to refuse to disclose and to prevent another person from disclosing a confidential communication made for the purpose of advice, diagnosis or treatment of his health condition between or among himself, his representative, and his physician or psychotherapist, and their representatives.

(2) Exceptions. There is no privilege under this Article in a criminal case as to a communication:

(a) When the communication is relevant to an issue of the health condition of the accused in any proceeding in which the accused relies upon the condition as an element of his defense.

(b) When the communication was intended to assist the patient or another person to commit or plan to commit what the patient knew or reasonably should have known to be a crime or fraud.

(c) When the communication was made in the course of an examination ordered by the court in a criminal case to determine the health condition of a patient, provided that a copy of the order was served on the patient prior to the communication.

(d) When the communication is a record of the results of a test for blood alcohol level or drugs taken from a patient who is under arrest, or who was subsequently arrested for an offense related to the test.

(e) When the communication is in the form of a tangible object, including a bullet, that is removed from the body of a patient and which was in the body as a result of the crime charged.

(f) When the communication is relevant to an investigation of or prosecution for child abuse, elder abuse, or the abuse of persons with disabilities or persons who are incompetent.

D. Who may claim the privilege. In both civil and criminal proceedings, the privilege may be claimed by the patient or by his legal representative. The person who was the physician, psychotherapist, or health care provider or their representatives, at the time of the communication is presumed to have authority to claim the privilege on behalf of the patient or deceased patient.

E. Waiver. The exceptions to the privilege set forth in Paragraph B(2) shall constitute a waiver of the privilege only as to testimony at trial or to discovery of the privileged communication by one of the discovery methods authorized by Code of Civil Procedure Article 1421 et seq., or pursuant to R.S. 40:1299.96 or R.S. 13:3715.1.

F. Medical malpractice. (1) There shall be no health care provider-patient privilege in medical malpractice claims as defined in R.S. 40:1299.41 et seq. as to information directly and specifically related to the factual issues pertaining to the liability of a health care provider who is a named party in a pending lawsuit or medical review panel proceeding.

(2) In medical malpractice claims information about a patient's current treatment or physical condition may only be disclosed pursuant to testimony at trial, pursuant to one of the discovery methods authorized by Code of Civil Procedure Article 1421 et seq., pursuant to R.S. 40:1299.96 or R.S. 13:3715.1.

G. Sanctions. Any attorney who violates a provision of this Article shall be subject to sanctions by the court.

Acts 1992, No. 376, §1, eff. Jan. 1, 1993; Acts 1993, No. 988, §2; Acts 1995, No. 1250, §3; Acts 1997, No. 643, §1; Acts 1999, No. 747, §1; Acts 1999, No. 1309, §11, eff. Jan. 1, 2000; Acts 2001, No. 486, §6, eff. June 21, 2001; Acts 2014, No. 811, §32, eff. June 23, 2014.

Art. 511. Communications to clergymen

A. Definitions. As used in this Article:

(1) A "clergyman" is a minister, priest, rabbi, Christian Science practitioner, or other similar functionary of a religious organization, or an individual reasonably believed so to be by the person consulting him.

(2) A communication is "confidential" if it is made privately and not intended for further disclosure except to other persons present in furtherance of the purpose of the communication.

B. General rule of privilege. A person has a privilege to refuse to disclose and to prevent another person from disclosing a confidential communication by the person to a clergyman in his professional character as spiritual adviser.

C. Who may claim the privilege. The privilege may be claimed by the person or by his legal representative. The clergyman is presumed to have authority to claim the privilege on behalf of the person or deceased person.
Acts 1992, No. 376, §1, eff. Jan. 1, 1993; Acts 2003, No. 1187, §2.

Art. 512. Political vote

Every person has a privilege to refuse to disclose the tenor of his vote at a political election conducted by secret ballot unless the vote was cast illegally.
Acts 1992, No. 376, §1, eff. Jan. 1, 1993.

Art. 513. Trade secrets

A person has a privilege, which may be claimed by him or his agent or employee, to refuse to disclose, and to prevent another person from disclosing, a trade secret owned by him, if the allowance of the privilege will not tend to conceal fraud or otherwise work injustice. When disclosure is directed, the judge shall take such protective measure as the interests of the holder of the privilege and of the parties and the furtherance of justice may require.
Acts 1992, No. 376, §1, eff. Jan. 1, 1993.

Art. 514. Identity of informer

A. General rule of privilege. The United States, a state, or subdivision thereof has a privilege to refuse to disclose, and to protect another from required disclosure of, the identity of a person who has furnished information in order to assist in an investigation of a possible violation of a criminal law.

B. Who may claim the privilege. The privilege may be claimed by the prosecuting authority or an appropriate representative of the public entity to which the information was furnished.

C. Inapplicability of privilege. No privilege shall be recognized if:

(1) The informer appears as a witness for the government and testifies with respect to matters previously disclosed in confidence.

(2) The identity of the informer has been disclosed to those who have cause to resent the communication by either the informer or the prosecution, or in a civil case, a person with authority to claim the privilege.

(3) The party seeking to overcome the privilege clearly demonstrates that the interest of the government in preventing disclosure is substantially outweighed by exceptional circumstances such that the informer's testimony is essential to the preparation of the defense or to a fair determination on the issue of guilt or innocence.

(4) In a criminal case, the prosecution objects.

D. Order to disclose identity. If the court orders disclosure of the identity of an informer and the prosecution opposes the disclosure, the court:

(1) In a criminal case, shall enter one of the following orders exclusively:

(a) An order suppressing the evidence concerning which the identity of the informer has been ordered.

(b) An order declaring a mistrial.

(2) In a civil case, may make any order justice requires.

Added by Acts 1995, No. 1040, §1.

Art. 515. Accountant-client privilege

A. Definitions. As used in this Article:

(1) "Client" is a person, including a public officer, corporation, partnership, unincorporated association, or other organization or entity, public or private, to whom professional services are rendered by an accountant, or who consults an accountant with a view to obtaining professional services from the accountant.

(2) "Representative of the client" is either of the following:

(a) A person having authority to obtain professional services from an accountant, or to act on advice so obtained, on behalf of the client.

(b) Any other person who makes or receives a confidential communication for the purpose of effectuating representation by an accountant for the client, while acting in the scope of employment for the client.

(3) "Accountant" is the holder of a license issued pursuant to the Louisiana Accountancy Act and shall include all persons and entities within the definition of licensee in R.S. 37:73(8).

(4) "Representative of the accountant" means a person engaged by the accountant to assist the accountant in the accountant's rendition of professional services.

(5) "Confidential communication" is any communication not intended to be disclosed to persons other than:

(a) Those to whom disclosure is made in furtherance of obtaining or rendering professional accounting services for the client.

(b) Those reasonably necessary for the transmission of the communication.

(c) When special circumstances warrant, those who are present at the behest of the client and are reasonably necessary to facilitate the communication.

B. General rule of privilege. A client has a privilege to refuse to disclose, and to prevent another person from disclosing, a confidential communication, whether oral, written, or otherwise, made for the purpose of facilitating the rendition of professional accounting services to the client, as well as the perceptions, observations, and the like, of the mental, emotional, or physical condition of the client in connection with such a communication. This privilege includes the protection of other confidential information or material obtained by the accountant from the client for the purpose of rendering professional services. This privilege exists when the communication is:

(1) Between the client or a representative of the client and the client's accountant or a representative of the accountant.

(2) Between the accountant and a representative of the accountant.

(3) By the client or his accountant or a representative of either, to an accountant or lawyer, or representative of an accountant or lawyer, who represents another party concerning a matter of common interest.

(4) Between representatives of the client or between the client and a representative of the client.

(5) Among accountants and their representatives representing the same client.

(6) Between representatives of the client's accountant.

C. Exceptions. There is no privilege under this Article as to a communication:

(1)(a) If the services of the accountant were sought or obtained to enable or aid anyone to commit or plan to commit what the client or his representative knew or reasonably should have known to be a crime or fraud.

(b) Made in furtherance of a crime or fraud.

(2) Which was with a client now deceased relevant to an issue between parties who claim through that decedent, regardless of whether the claims are by testate or intestate succession or by transaction inter vivos.

(3) Which is relevant to an issue of breach of duty by an accountant to the client or by a client to the client's accountant.

(4)(a) Which is relevant to an issue of authenticity or capacity concerning a document which the accountant signed as a witness or notary.

(b) Concerning the testimony of a representative of an accountant regarding a communication relevant to an issue of authenticity or capacity concerning a document to which the representative is a witness or notary.

(5) Which is relevant to a matter of common interest between or among two or more clients if the communication was made by any of them or their representative to an accountant or his representative retained or consulted in common, when subsequently offered by one client against the other in a civil action.

(6) Concerning the identity of the accountant's client or his representative, unless disclosure of the identity by the accountant or his representative would reveal either the reason for which accounting services were sought or a communication which is otherwise privileged under this Article.

(7) Concerning information required to be disclosed by the standards of the public accounting profession in reporting on the examination of financial statements whose proceedings are protected from discovery pursuant to R.S. 37:86.

(8) Concerning disclosures in investigations or proceedings of the State Board of Certified Public Accountants of Louisiana pursuant to the provisions of Part I of the Louisiana Accountancy Act whose proceedings are protected from discovery pursuant to R.S. 37:86.

(9) Concerning disclosures in ethical investigations of an accountant conducted by private professional organizations whose proceedings are protected from discovery pursuant to R.S. 37:86 or in the course of quality or peer reviews.

(10) In any domestic proceeding including the partition of community property and the settlement of claims arising from matrimonial regimes, spousal support, and child support.

D. Who may claim privilege. The privilege may be claimed by the client, the client's agent or accountant, or the successor, trustee, or similar representative of a client that is a corporation, partnership, unincorporated association, or other organization, whether or not in existence. The person who was the accountant or the accountant's representative at the time of the communication is presumed to have authority to claim the privilege on behalf of the client, former client, or deceased client.

    E. Scope. Nothing in this Article is intended to affect the absolute privileges against disclosure contained in R.S. 37:86(B) through (E).

Acts 2001, No. 954, §1; Acts 2003, No. 152, §1.

Art. 516. Subpoena of accountant or his representative in criminal cases

    A. General rule. Neither a subpoena nor a court order shall be issued to an accountant or his representative to appear or testify in any criminal investigation or proceeding when the purpose of the subpoena or order is to ask the accountant or his representative to reveal information about a client or former client obtained in the course of representing the client unless the party issuing the subpoena executes and attaches to the subpoena an affidavit that:

    (1) The information sought is essential to the successful completion of an ongoing investigation, prosecution, or defense.

    (2) The purpose of seeking the information is not to harass the accountant or the client.

    (3) With respect to a subpoena, the subpoena lists the information sought with particularity, is reasonably limited as to subject matter and period of time, and gives timely notice.

    (4) There is no practicable alternative means of obtaining the information.

    B. Waiver. Failure to object timely to noncompliance with the terms of this Article constitutes a waiver of the procedural protections of this Article, but does not constitute a waiver of any privilege.

    C. Binding effect of determination; notice to client. The determination that an accountant-client privilege is not applicable to the testimony shall not bind the client or former client unless the client or former client was given notice of the subpoena.

    D. Exceptions. This Article shall not apply in habitual offender proceedings when an accountant is called as a witness for purposes of identification of his client or former client.

    E. Scope. Nothing in this Article is intended to affect the absolute privileges against disclosure contained in R.S. 37:86(B) through (E).

    Acts 2001, No. 954, §1.

Art. 517. Subpoena of accountant; civil, juvenile, administrative proceedings

    A. General rule. Neither a subpoena nor a court order shall be issued to an accountant or his representative to appear or testify in any civil or juvenile proceeding, including pretrial discovery, or in an administrative investigation or hearing, except proceedings by the State Board of Accountancy as provided in the Louisiana Accountancy Act, where the purpose of the subpoena or order is to ask the accountant or his representative to reveal information about a client or former client obtained in the course of representing the client unless the court determines, after a contradictory hearing held after service of actual notice to the accountant and the client at least ten days prior to the contradictory hearing, that the information sought is not protected from disclosure by any applicable privilege or work product rule and all of the following apply:

(1) The information sought is essential to the successful completion of an ongoing investigation, is essential to the case of the party seeking the information, and is not merely peripheral, cumulative, or speculative.

(2) The purpose of seeking the information is not to harass the accountant or his client.

(3) With respect to a subpoena, the subpoena lists the information sought with particularity, is reasonably limited as to subject matter and period of time, and gives timely notice.

(4) There is no practicable alternative means of obtaining the information.

B. Waiver. Failure to object timely to noncompliance with the terms of this Article constitutes a waiver of the procedural protections of this Article, but does not constitute a waiver of any privilege.

C. Binding effect of determination; notice to client. The determination that an accountant-client privilege is not applicable to the testimony shall not bind the client or former client unless the client or former client was given notice within the time period set forth in Subsection A of this Section, of the time, place, and substance of the hearing and had an opportunity fully to participate in that hearing.

D. Scope. Nothing in this Article is intended to affect the absolute privileges against disclosure in R.S. 37:86(B) through (E).
Acts 2001, No. 954, §1.

Art. 518. Trained peer support member privilege

A.(1) A trained peer support member shall not, without consent of the emergency responder making the communication, be compelled to testify about any communication made to the trained peer support member by the emergency responder while receiving peer support services. The trained peer support member shall be designated as such by the emergency service agency or entity, prior to the incident that results in receiving peer support services. The privilege only applies when the communication was made to the trained peer support member.

(2) The privilege does not apply to any of the following if:

(a) The trained peer support member was an initial responding emergency responder, a witness, or a party to the incident which prompted the delivery of peer support services to the emergency responder.

(b) A communication reveals the intended commission of a crime or harmful act and such disclosure is determined to be necessary by the trained peer support member to protect any person from a clear, imminent risk of serious mental or physical harm or injury, or to forestall a serious threat to the public safety.

B. For purposes of this Section, a "trained peer support member" is an emergency responder or civilian volunteer of an emergency service agency or entity, who has received training in Critical Incident Stress Management to provide emotional and moral support to an emergency responder who needs those services as a result of an incident in which the emergency responder was involved while acting in his official capacity. A "trained peer support member" also includes a volunteer counselor or other mental health services provider who has been designated by the emergency service agency or entity to provide emotional and moral support and counseling to an emergency responder who needs those services as a result of an incident in which the emergency responder was involved while acting in his official capacity.
Acts 2003, No. 1137, §1.

Art. 519. Subpoena of judge or his representative in civil and criminal cases

A. General rule. Neither a subpoena nor a court order shall be issued to a judge or his representative to appear or testify in any civil, criminal, or juvenile proceeding, including pretrial discovery or an administrative hearing, unless, after a contradictory hearing, it has been determined that the information sought is not protected from disclosure by the judicial deliberative process privilege, and all of the following:

(1) The information sought is essential to the case of the party seeking the information and is not merely peripheral, cumulative, or speculative.

(2) The purpose of seeking the information is not to harass the judge, nor for the mere purpose of seeking recusal of the judge.

(3) With respect to a subpoena, the subpoena lists the information sought with particularity, is reasonably limited as to subject matter and period of time, and gives timely notice.

(4) There is no practical alternative means of obtaining the information.

B. Waiver. Failure to object timely to a party's non-compliance with the provisions of this Article constitutes a waiver of the procedural protections of this Article, but does not constitute a waiver of any privilege.

C. The procedural provisions of and the protections afforded by Paragraph A of this Article shall extend to any judge of any court provided for by Article V of the Constitution of Louisiana and to any commissioner or special master of such court.

Acts 2012, No. 563, §1, eff. June 5, 2012.

CHAPTER 6. WITNESSES

Art. 601. General rule of competency

Every person of proper understanding is competent to be a witness except as otherwise provided by legislation.
Acts 1988, No. 515, §1, eff. Jan. 1, 1989.

Art. 602. Lack of personal knowledge

A witness may not testify to a matter unless evidence is introduced sufficient to support a finding that he has personal knowledge of the matter. Evidence to prove personal knowledge may, but need not, consist of the testimony of the witness himself. This Article is subject to the provisions of Article 703, relating to opinion testimony by expert witnesses.
Acts 1988, No. 515, §1, eff. Jan. 1, 1989.

Art. 603. Oath or affirmation

Before testifying, every witness shall be required to declare that he will testify truthfully, by oath or affirmation administered in a form calculated to awaken his conscience and impress his mind with his duty to do so.
Acts 1988, No. 515, §1, eff. Jan. 1, 1989.

Art. 604. Interpreters

An interpreter is subject to the provisions of this Code relating to qualification as an expert and the administration of an oath or affirmation that he will make a true translation.
Acts 1988, No. 515, §1, eff. Jan. 1, 1989.

Art. 605. Disqualification of judge as witness

The judge presiding at the trial may not testify in that trial as a witness. No objection need be made in order to preserve the point.
Acts 1988, No. 515, §1, eff. Jan. 1, 1989.

Art. 606. Disqualification of juror as witness

A. At the trial. A member of the jury may not testify as a witness before that jury in the trial of the case in which he is sitting as a juror. If he is called so to testify, the opposing party shall be afforded an opportunity to object out of the presence of the jury.

B. Inquiry into validity of verdict or indictment. Upon an inquiry into the validity of a verdict or indictment, a juror may not testify as to any matter or statement occurring during the course of the jury's deliberations or to the effect of anything upon his or any other juror's mind or emotions as influencing him to assent to or dissent from the verdict or indictment or concerning his mental processes in connection therewith, except that a juror may testify on the question whether any outside influence was improperly brought to bear upon any juror, and, in criminal cases only, whether extraneous prejudicial information was improperly brought to the jury's

attention. Nor may his affidavit or evidence of any statement by him concerning a matter about which he would be precluded from testifying be received for these purposes.
Acts 1988, No. 515, §1, eff. Jan. 1, 1989.

Art. 607. Attacking and supporting credibility generally

A. Who may attack credibility. The credibility of a witness may be attacked by any party, including the party calling him.

B. Time for attacking and supporting credibility. The credibility of a witness may not be attacked until the witness has been sworn, and the credibility of a witness may not be supported unless it has been attacked. However, a party may question any witness as to his relationship to the parties, interest in the lawsuit, or capacity to perceive or to recollect.

C. Attacking credibility intrinsically. Except as otherwise provided by legislation, a party, to attack the credibility of a witness, may examine him concerning any matter having a reasonable tendency to disprove the truthfulness or accuracy of his testimony.

D. Attacking credibility extrinsically. Except as otherwise provided by legislation:

(1) Extrinsic evidence to show a witness' bias, interest, corruption, or defect of capacity is admissible to attack the credibility of the witness.

(2) Other extrinsic evidence, including prior inconsistent statements and evidence contradicting the witness' testimony, is admissible when offered solely to attack the credibility of a witness unless the court determines that the probative value of the evidence on the issue of credibility is substantially outweighed by the risks of undue consumption of time, confusion of the issues, or unfair prejudice.
Acts 1988, No. 515, §1, eff. Jan. 1, 1989.

Art. 608. Attacking or supporting credibility by character evidence

A. Reputation evidence of character. The credibility of a witness may be attacked or supported by evidence in the form of general reputation only, but subject to these limitations:

(1) The evidence may refer only to character for truthfulness or untruthfulness.

(2) A foundation must first be established that the character witness is familiar with the reputation of the witness whose credibility is in issue. The character witness shall not express his personal opinion as to the character of the witness whose credibility is in issue.

(3) Inquiry into specific acts on direct examination while qualifying the character witness or otherwise is prohibited.

B. Particular acts, vices, or courses of conduct. Particular acts, vices, or courses of conduct of a witness may not be inquired into or proved by extrinsic evidence for the purpose of attacking his character for truthfulness, other than conviction of crime as provided in Articles 609 and 609.1 or as constitutionally required.

C. Cross-examination of character witnesses. A witness who has testified to the character for truthfulness or untruthfulness of another witness may be cross-examined as to whether he has heard about particular acts of that witness bearing upon his credibility.
Acts 1988, No. 515, §1, eff. Jan. 1, 1989.

Art. 609. Attacking credibility by evidence of conviction of crime in civil cases

A. General civil rule. For the purpose of attacking the credibility of a witness in civil cases, no evidence of the details of the crime of which he was convicted is admissible. However, evidence of the name of the crime of which he was convicted and the date of conviction is admissible if the crime:

(1) Was punishable by death or imprisonment in excess of six months under the law under which he was convicted, and the court determines that the probative value of admitting this evidence outweighs its prejudicial effect to a party; or

(2) Involved dishonesty or false statement, regardless of the punishment.

B. Time limit. Evidence of a conviction under this Article is not admissible if a period of more than ten years has elapsed since the date of the conviction.

C. Effect of pardon or annulment. Evidence of a conviction is not admissible under this Article if the conviction has been the subject of a pardon, annulment, or other equivalent procedure explicitly based on a finding of innocence.

D. Juvenile adjudications. Evidence of juvenile adjudications of delinquency is generally not admissible under this Article.

E. Pendency of appeal. The pendency of an appeal therefrom does not render evidence of a conviction inadmissible. When evidence of a conviction is admissible, evidence of the pendency of an appeal is also admissible.

F. Arrest, indictment, or prosecution. Evidence of the arrest, indictment, or prosecution of a witness is not admissible for the purpose of attacking his credibility.
Acts 1988, No. 515, §1, eff. Jan. 1, 1989.

Art. 609.1. Attacking credibility by evidence of conviction of crime in criminal cases

A. General criminal rule. In a criminal case, every witness by testifying subjects himself to examination relative to his criminal convictions, subject to limitations set forth below.

B. Convictions. Generally, only offenses for which the witness has been convicted are admissible upon the issue of his credibility, and no inquiry is permitted into matters for which there has only been an arrest, the issuance of an arrest warrant, an indictment, a prosecution, or an acquittal.

C. Details of convictions. Ordinarily, only the fact of a conviction, the name of the offense, the date thereof, and the sentence imposed is admissible. However, details of the offense may become admissible to show the true nature of the offense:

(1) When the witness has denied the conviction or denied recollection thereof;

(2) When the witness has testified to exculpatory facts or circumstances surrounding the conviction; or

(3) When the probative value thereof outweighs the danger of unfair prejudice, confusion of the issues, or misleading the jury.

D. Effect of pending post-conviction relief procedures. The pendency of an appeal or other post-conviction relief procedures does not render the conviction inadmissible, but may be introduced as bearing upon the weight to be given the evidence of the conviction.

E. Effect of pardon or annulment. When a pardon or annulment, based upon a finding of innocence, has been granted, evidence of that conviction is not admissible to attack the credibility of the witness.

F. Juvenile adjudications. Evidence of juvenile adjudications of delinquency is generally not admissible under this Article, except for use in proceedings brought pursuant to the habitual offender law, R.S. 15:529.1.

Acts 1988, No. 515, §1, eff. Jan. 1, 1989; Acts 1994, 3rd Ex. Sess., No. 23, §3.

Art 610. Religious beliefs or opinions

Except as provided in Article 613, evidence of the beliefs or opinions of a witness on matters of religion is not admissible for the sole purpose of showing that by reason of their nature his credibility is impaired or enhanced.

Acts 1988, No. 515, §1, eff. Jan. 1, 1989.

Art. 611. Mode and order of interrogation and presentation

A. Control by court. Except as provided by this Article and Code of Criminal Procedure Article 773, the parties to a proceeding have the primary responsibility of presenting the evidence and examining the witnesses. The court, however, shall exercise reasonable control over the mode and order of interrogating witnesses and presenting evidence so as to:

(1) Make the interrogation and presentation effective for the ascertainment of the truth;

(2) Avoid needless consumption of time; and

(3) Protect witnesses from harassment or undue embarrassment.

B. Scope of cross-examination. A witness may be cross-examined on any matter relevant to any issue in the case, including credibility. However, in a civil case, when a party or person identified with a party has been called as a witness by an adverse party to testify only as to particular aspects of the case, the court shall limit the scope of cross-examination to matters testified to on direct examination, unless the interests of justice otherwise require.

C. Leading questions. Generally, leading questions should not be used on the direct examination of a witness except as may be necessary to develop his testimony and in examining an expert witness on his opinions and inferences. However, when a party calls a hostile witness, a witness who is unable or unwilling to respond to proper questioning, an adverse party, or a witness identified with an adverse party, interrogation may be by leading questions. Generally, leading questions should be permitted on cross-examination. However, the court ordinarily shall prohibit counsel for a party from using leading questions when that party or a person identified with him is examined by his counsel, even when the party or a person identified with him has been called as a witness by another party and tendered for cross-examination.

D. Scope of redirect examination; recross examination. A witness who has been cross-examined is subject to redirect examination as to matters covered on cross-examination and, in the discretion of the court, as to other matters in the case. When the court has allowed a party to bring out new matter on redirect, the other parties shall be provided an opportunity to recross on such matters.

E. Rebuttal evidence. The plaintiff in a civil case and the state in a criminal prosecution shall have the right to rebut evidence adduced by their opponents.
Acts 1988, No. 515, §1, eff. Jan. 1, 1989.

Art. 612. Writing used to refresh memory

A. Civil cases. In a civil case, any writing, recording, or object may be used by a witness to refresh his memory while testifying. If a witness asserts that his memory is refreshed he must then testify from memory independent of the writing, recording, or object. If, before or during testimony, a witness has used or uses a writing, recording, or object to refresh his memory for the purpose of testifying in court, an adverse party is entitled, subject to Paragraph C, to have the writing, recording, or object produced, if practicable, at the hearing, to inspect it, to examine the witness thereon, and to introduce in evidence those portions which relate to the testimony of the witness. If production of the writing, recording, or object at the hearing is impracticable, the court may make any appropriate order, including one for inspection.

B. Criminal cases. In a criminal case, any writing, recording, or object may be used by a witness to refresh his memory while testifying. If a witness asserts that his memory is refreshed he must then testify from memory independent of the writing, recording, or object. If while testifying a witness uses a writing, recording, or object to refresh his memory an adverse party is entitled, subject to Paragraph C, to inspect it, to examine the witness thereon, and to introduce in evidence those portions which relate to the testimony of the witness.

C. Claim of irrelevance. If it is claimed that a writing or recording contains matters not related to the subject matter of the testimony the court shall examine it in camera, excise any portions not so related, and order delivery of the remainder to the party entitled thereto. Any portion withheld over objections shall be preserved and made available to the appellate court in the event of an appeal.

D. Failure to produce. If a writing, recording, or object is not produced or delivered pursuant to an order under this Article, the court shall make any order justice requires, except that in criminal cases when the prosecution elects not to comply, the order shall only be one excluding the testimony or, if the court in its discretion determines that the interests of justice so require, declaring a mistrial.
Acts 1988, No. 515, §1, eff. Jan. 1, 1989.

Art. 613. Foundation for extrinsic attack on credibility

Except as the interests of justice otherwise require, extrinsic evidence of bias, interest, or corruption, prior inconsistent statements, conviction of crime, or defects of capacity is admissible after the proponent has first fairly directed the witness' attention to the statement, act, or matter alleged, and the witness has been given the opportunity to admit the fact and has failed distinctly to do so.
Acts 1988, No. 515, §1, eff. Jan. 1, 1989.

Art. 614. Calling and questioning of witnesses by court
        A. Calling by court. The court, at the request of a party or if otherwise authorized by legislation, may call witnesses, and all parties are entitled to examine witnesses thus called.
        B. Questioning by court. The court may question witnesses, whether called by itself or by a party.
        C. Objections. Objections to the calling of witnesses by the court or to questioning of witnesses by it may be made at the time or at the next available opportunity when the jury is not present.
        D. Exception. In a jury trial, the court may not call or examine a witness, except upon the express consent of all parties, which consent shall not be requested within the hearing of the jury.
Acts 1988, No. 515, §1, eff. Jan. 1, 1989.

Art. 615. Exclusion of witnesses
        A. As a matter of right. On its own motion the court may, and on request of a party the court shall, order that the witnesses be excluded from the courtroom or from a place where they can see or hear the proceedings, and refrain from discussing the facts of the case with anyone other than counsel in the case. In the interests of justice, the court may exempt any witness from its order of exclusion.
        B. Exceptions. This Article does not authorize exclusion of any of the following:
        (1) A party who is a natural person.
        (2) A single officer or single employee of a party which is not a natural person designated as its representative or case agent by its attorney.
        (3) A person whose presence is shown by a party to be essential to the presentation of his cause such as an expert.
        (4) The victim of the offense or the family of the victim.
        C. Violation of exclusion order. A court may impose appropriate sanctions for violations of its exclusion order including contempt, appropriate instructions to the jury, or when such sanctions are insufficient, disqualification of the witness.
Acts 1988, No. 515, §1, eff. Jan. 1, 1989; Acts 1999, No. 783, §2, eff. Jan. 1, 2000.

CHAPTER 7. OPINIONS AND EXPERT TESTIMONY

Art. 701. Opinion testimony by lay witnesses

If the witness is not testifying as an expert, his testimony in the form of opinions or inferences is limited to those opinions or inferences which are:

(1) Rationally based on the perception of the witness; and

(2) Helpful to a clear understanding of his testimony or the determination of a fact in issue. Acts 1988, No. 515, §1, eff. Jan. 1, 1989.

Art. 702. Testimony by experts

A. A witness who is qualified as an expert by knowledge, skill, experience, training, or education may testify in the form of an opinion or otherwise if:

(1) The expert's scientific, technical, or other specialized knowledge will help the trier of fact to understand the evidence or to determine a fact in issue;

(2) The testimony is based on sufficient facts or data;

(3) The testimony is the product of reliable principles and methods; and

(4) The expert has reliably applied the principles and methods to the facts of the case.

B. This Article shall also govern expert witnesses on the issue of memory and eyewitness identification. In a criminal case, if a party seeks to offer the testimony of a memory and eyewitness identification expert under this Article, such expert testimony may be considered for admission only if all provisions of Subparagraph A of this Article are satisfied. A memory and eyewitness identification expert's testimony may not be admitted under this Article if there is physical or scientific evidence that corroborates the eyewitness identification of the defendant. An expert's testimony admitted under this Paragraph shall not offer an opinion as to whether a witness's memory or eyewitness identification is accurate.

Acts 1988, No. 515, §1, eff. Jan. 1, 1989; Acts 2014, No. 630, §1; Acts 2019, No. 115.

NOTE: No changes in law or result in a ruling on evidence admissibility shall be presumed or is intended by the Legislature of Louisiana by the passage of Acts 2014, No. 630.

Art. 703. Bases of opinion testimony by experts

The facts or data in the particular case upon which an expert bases an opinion or inference may be those perceived by or made known to him at or before the hearing. If of a type reasonably relied upon by experts in the particular field in forming opinions or inferences upon the subject, the facts or data need not be admissible in evidence.

Acts 1988, No. 515, §1, eff. Jan. 1, 1989.

Art. 704. Opinion on ultimate issue

Testimony in the form of an opinion or inference otherwise admissible is not to be excluded solely because it embraces an ultimate issue to be decided by the trier of fact. However, in a criminal case, an expert witness shall not express an opinion as to the guilt or innocence of the accused.

Acts 1988, No. 515, §1, eff. Jan. 1, 1989.

Art. 705. Disclosure of facts or data underlying expert opinion; foundation

A. Civil cases. In a civil case, the expert may testify in terms of opinion or inference and give his reasons therefor without prior disclosure of the underlying facts or data, unless the court requires otherwise. The expert may in any event be required to disclose the underlying facts or data on cross-examination.

B. Criminal cases. In a criminal case, every expert witness must state the facts upon which his opinion is based, provided, however, that with respect to evidence which would otherwise be inadmissible such basis shall only be elicited on cross-examination.

Acts 1988, No. 515, §1, eff. Jan. 1, 1989.

Art. 706. Court appointed experts

A. Civil cases. In a civil case, the court may on its own motion or on the motion of any party enter an order to show cause why expert witnesses should not be appointed, and may request the parties to submit nominations. The court may appoint any expert witnesses agreed upon by the parties, and may appoint expert witnesses of its own selection. An expert witness shall not be appointed by the court unless he consents to act. A witness so appointed shall be informed of his duties by the court in writing, a copy of which shall be filed with the clerk, or at a conference in which the parties shall have opportunity to participate. A witness so appointed shall advise the parties of his findings, if any; his deposition may be taken by any party; and he may be called to testify by the court or any party.

B. Disclosure of appointment. In a civil case, in the exercise of its discretion, the court may authorize disclosure to the jury of the fact that the court appointed the expert witness.

C. Parties' experts of own selection. Nothing in this Article limits the parties in calling expert witnesses of their own selection.

D. Criminal cases. In a criminal case, the court may appoint an expert witness only when specifically authorized by statute, or as constitutionally required.

Acts 1988, No. 515, §1, eff. Jan. 1, 1989.

CHAPTER 8. HEARSAY

Art. 801. Definitions

The following definitions apply under this Chapter:

A. Statement. A "statement" is:

(1) An oral or written assertion; or

(2) Nonverbal conduct of a person, if it is intended by him as an assertion.

B. Declarant. A "declarant" is a person who makes a statement.

C. Hearsay. "Hearsay" is a statement, other than one made by the declarant while testifying at the present trial or hearing, offered in evidence to prove the truth of the matter asserted.

D. Statements which are not hearsay. A statement is not hearsay if:

(1) Prior statement by witness. The declarant testifies at the trial or hearing and is subject to cross-examination concerning the statement, and the statement is:

(a) In a criminal case, inconsistent with his testimony, provided that the proponent has first fairly directed the witness' attention to the statement and the witness has been given the opportunity to admit the fact and where there exists any additional evidence to corroborate the matter asserted by the prior inconsistent statement;

(b) Consistent with his testimony and is offered to rebut an express or implied charge against him of recent fabrication or improper influence or motive;

(c) One of identification of a person made after perceiving the person;

(d) Consistent with the declarant's testimony and is one of initial complaint of sexually assaultive behavior; or

(e) A statement made by the victim of a sexually-oriented criminal offense to a healthcare provider during the course of a forensic medical examination as defined in R.S. 15:622 and the healthcare provider has documented that statement in writing during the course of the forensic medical examination.

(2) Personal, adoptive, and authorized admissions. The statement is offered against a party and is:

(a) His own statement, in either his individual or a representative capacity;

(b) A statement of which he has manifested his adoption or belief in its truth; or

(c) A statement by a person authorized by him to make a statement concerning the subject.

(3) Relational and privity admissions. The statement is offered against a party, and the statement is:

(a) A statement by an agent or employee of the party against whom it is offered, concerning a matter within the scope of his agency or employment, made during the existence of the relationship;

(b) A statement by a declarant while participating in a conspiracy to commit a crime or civil wrong and in furtherance of the objective of the conspiracy, provided that a prima facie case of conspiracy is established;

(c) In a civil case, a statement by a declarant when the liability, obligation, or duty of the party against whom it is offered is derivatively based in whole or in part upon a liability, obligation, or duty of the declarant, or when the claim or right asserted by that party is barred or diminished by a breach of duty by the declarant, and when the statement would be admissible if offered against the declarant as a party in an action involving that liability, obligation, or breach of duty;

(d) In a civil case, a statement by a declarant when a right, title, or interest in any property or claim asserted by the party against whom it is offered requires a determination that a right, title, or interest exists or existed in the declarant during the time that that party now claims the declarant was the holder of the right, title, or interest, and when the statement would be admissible if offered against the declarant as a party in an action involving that right, title, or interest;

(e) A statement by a declarant offered against the party in an action for damages arising from the death of that declarant; or

(f) A statement by a minor child offered against a party in an action to recover for injury to that child, or against the person responsible for the child in an action to recover damages for losses caused by the child.

(4) Things said or done. The statements are events speaking for themselves under the immediate pressure of the occurrence, through the instructive, impulsive and spontaneous words and acts of the participants, and not the words of the participants when narrating the events, and which are necessary incidents of the criminal act, or immediate concomitants of it, or form in conjunction with it one continuous transaction.

E. Optical Disk Imaging System. "Optical disk imaging system" means a storage system that utilizes non-erasable Write Once Read Many (WORM) optical storage technology to record information on an optical disk with the use of laser technology, and that utilizes laser technology to retrieve and read previously stored information.

Acts 1988, No. 515, §1, eff. Jan. 1, 1989; Acts 1995, No. 346, §1; Acts 1995, No. 1300, §1; Acts 2004, No. 694, §1; Acts 2019, No. 115.

Art. 802. Hearsay rule

Hearsay is not admissible except as otherwise provided by this Code or other legislation.
Acts 1988, No. 515, §1, eff. Jan. 1, 1989.

Art. 803. Hearsay exceptions; availability of declarant immaterial

The following are not excluded by the hearsay rule, even though the declarant is available as a witness:

(1) Present sense impression. A statement describing or explaining an event or condition made while the declarant was perceiving the event or condition, or immediately thereafter.

(2) Excited utterance. A statement relating to a startling event or condition made while the declarant was under the stress of excitement caused by the event or condition.

(3) Then existing mental, emotional, or physical condition. A statement of the declarant's then existing state of mind, emotion, sensation, or physical condition (such as intent, plan, motive, design, mental feeling, pain, and bodily health), offered to prove the declarant's then existing condition or his future action. A statement of memory or belief, however, is not admissible to prove the fact remembered or believed unless it relates to the execution, revocation, identification, or terms of declarant's testament.

(4) Statements for purposes of medical treatment and medical diagnosis in connection with treatment. Statements made for purposes of medical treatment and medical diagnosis in connection with treatment and describing medical history, or past or present symptoms, pain, or sensations, or the inception or general character of the cause or external source thereof insofar as reasonably pertinent to treatment or diagnosis in connection with treatment.

(5) Recorded recollection. A memorandum or record concerning a matter about which a witness once had knowledge but now has insufficient recollection to enable him to testify fully and accurately, shown to have been made or adopted by the witness when the matter was fresh in his memory and to reflect that knowledge correctly. If admitted, the memorandum or record may be read into evidence and received as an exhibit but may not itself be taken into the jury room. This exception is subject to the provisions of Article 612.

(6) Records of regularly conducted business activity. A memorandum, report, record, or data compilation, in any form, including but not limited to that which is stored by the use of an optical disk imaging system, of acts, events, conditions, opinions, or diagnoses, made at or near the time by, or from information transmitted by, a person with knowledge, if made and kept in the course of a regularly conducted business activity, and if it was the regular practice of that business activity to make and to keep the memorandum, report, record, or data compilation, all as shown by the testimony of the custodian or other qualified witness, unless the source of information or the method or circumstances of preparation indicate lack of trustworthiness. This exception is inapplicable unless the recorded information was furnished to the business either by a person who was routinely acting for the business in reporting the information or in circumstances under which the statement would not be excluded by the hearsay rule. The term "business" as used in this Paragraph includes business, institution, association, profession, occupation, and calling of every kind, whether or not conducted for profit. Public records and reports which are specifically excluded from the public records exception by Article 803(8)(b) shall not qualify as an exception to the hearsay rule under this Paragraph.

(7) Absence of entry in records of regularly conducted business activity. Evidence that a matter is not included in the memoranda, reports, records, or data compilations, in any form, kept in accordance with the provisions of Paragraph (6), to prove the nonoccurrence or nonexistence of the matter, if the matter was of a kind of which a memorandum, report, record, or data compilation was regularly made and preserved unless the sources of information or other circumstances indicate lack of trustworthiness.

(8) Public records and reports. (a) Records, reports, statements, or data compilations, in any form, of a public office or agency setting forth:

(i) Its regularly conducted and regularly recorded activities;

(ii) Matters observed pursuant to duty imposed by law and as to which there was a duty to report; or

(iii) Factual findings resulting from an investigation made pursuant to authority granted by law. Factual findings are conclusions of fact reached by a governmental agency and may be based upon information furnished to it by persons other than agents and employees of that agency.

(b) Except as specifically provided otherwise by legislation, the following are excluded from this exception to the hearsay rule:

(i) Investigative reports by police and other law enforcement personnel or the notification of administrative sanctions form which records the administrative sanctions proceedings conducted pursuant to Code of Criminal Procedure Article 899.1 or R.S. 15:574.7.

(ii) Investigative reports prepared by or for any government, public office, or public agency when offered by that or any other government, public office, or public agency in a case in which it is a party.

(iii) Factual findings offered by the prosecution in a criminal case.

(iv) Factual findings resulting from investigation of a particular complaint, case, or incident, including an investigation into the facts and circumstances on which the present proceeding is based or an investigation into a similar occurrence or occurrences.

(9) Records of vital statistics. Records or data compilations, in any form, of birth, filiation, adoption, or death, including fetal death, still birth, and abortion, or of marital status, including divorce and annulment, if the report thereof was made to a public office pursuant to requirements of law, and any record included within the Louisiana Vital Statistics Laws.

(10) Absence of public record or entry. To prove the absence of a record, report, statement, or data compilation, in any form, or the nonoccurrence or nonexistence of a matter of which a record, report, statement, or data compilation, in any form, was regularly made and preserved by a public office or agency, evidence in the form of a certification in accordance with Article 902, or testimony, that diligent search failed to disclose the record, report, statement, or data compilation, or entry.

(11) Records of religious organizations. Statements of births, marriages, divorces, deaths, filiation, ancestry, relationship by blood or marriage, or other similar facts of personal or family history, contained in a regularly kept record of a religious organization.

(12) Marriage, baptismal, and similar certificates. Statements of fact contained in a certificate that the maker performed a marriage or other ceremony or administered a sacrament, made by a clergyman, public official, or other person authorized by the rules or practices of a religious organization or by law to perform the act certified, and purporting to have been issued at the time of the act or within a reasonable time thereafter.

(13) Family records. Statements of fact concerning personal or family history contained in family Bibles, genealogies, charts, engravings on rings, inscriptions on family portraits, engravings on urns, crypts, or tombstones, or the like.

(14) Records of documents affecting an interest in property. Records of documents purporting to establish or affect an interest in property to the extent that their admission is authorized by other legislation.

(15) Statements in documents affecting an interest in property. A statement contained in a document purporting to establish or affect an interest in property if the matter stated was relevant to the purpose of the document, unless dealings with the property since the document was made have been inconsistent with the truth of the statement or the purport of the document.

(16) Statements in ancient documents. Statements in a document in existence thirty years or more the authenticity of which is established, or statements in a recorded document as provided by other legislation.

(17) Market reports, commercial publications. Market quotations, tabulations, lists, directories, or other published compilations, generally used and relied upon by the public or by persons in particular occupations.

(18) Learned treatises. To the extent called to the attention of an expert witness upon cross-examination or, in a civil case, relied upon by him in direct examination, statements contained in published treatises, periodicals, or pamphlets on a subject of history, medicine, or other science or art, established as a reliable authority by the testimony or admission of the witness or by other expert testimony or by judicial notice. If admitted, such a statement may be read into evidence and received as an exhibit but may not be taken into the jury room.

(19) Reputation concerning personal or family history. Reputation, arising before the controversy, among members of his family by blood, adoption, or marriage, or among his associates, or in the community, concerning a person's birth, adoption, marriage, divorce, death,

filiation, relationship by blood, adoption, or marriage, ancestry, or other similar fact of his personal or family history.

(20) Reputation concerning boundaries or general history. Reputation in a community, arising before the controversy, as to boundaries of or customs affecting lands in the community, and reputation as to events of general history important to the community or state or nation in which located.

(21) Reputation as to character. Reputation of a person's character among his associates or in the community.

(22) Judgment of previous conviction. Evidence of a final judgment, entered after a trial or upon a plea of guilty (but not upon a plea of nolo contendere), adjudging a person guilty of a crime punishable by death or imprisonment in excess of six months, to prove any fact essential to sustain the judgment. This exception does not permit the prosecutor in a criminal prosecution to offer as evidence the judgment of conviction of a person other than the accused, except for the purpose of attacking the credibility of a witness. The pendency of an appeal may be shown but does not affect admissibility.

(23) Judgment as to personal, family, or general history, or boundaries. Judgments as proof of matters of personal, family, or general history, or boundaries, essential to the judgment, if the same would be provable by evidence of reputation.

(24) Testimony as to age. A witness' testimony as to his own age.

Acts 1988, No. 515, §1, eff. Jan. 1, 1989; Acts 1995, No. 346, §1; Acts 1995, No. 1300, §1; Acts 2004, No. 26, §4; Acts 2012, No. 158, §1.

Art. 803.1. Hearsay exceptions; foreign records of regularly conducted activity

A.(1) Except as otherwise provided by this Code, in a criminal proceeding, a foreign record of regularly conducted activity, or a copy of such record, shall not be excluded as evidence by the hearsay rule if a foreign certification attests to the following:

(a) Such record was made, at or near the time of the occurrence of the matters set forth, by or from information transmitted by, a person with knowledge of those matters; and

(b) Such record was kept in the course of a regularly conducted business activity; and

(c) The business activity made such a record as a regular practice; and

(d) If such record is not the original, such record is a duplicate of the original, unless the source of information or the method or circumstances of preparation indicate lack of trustworthiness.

(2) A party intending to offer in evidence pursuant to this Article a foreign record of regularly conducted activity shall provide written notice of that intention to each other party not less than ten days prior to trial. A motion opposing admission in evidence of such record shall be made by the opposing party and determined by the court before trial. Failure by a party to file such motion before trial shall constitute a waiver of objection to such record or duplicate, but the court for cause shown may grant relief from the waiver.

B. As used in this Article:

(1) "Foreign record of regularly conducted activity" means a memorandum, report, record, or data compilation, in any form, of acts, events, conditions, opinions, or diagnoses, maintained by a business domiciled in a jurisdiction outside the territorial limits of the state of Louisiana.

(2) "Foreign certification" means a written declaration made and signed in a jurisdiction outside the territorial limits of the state of Louisiana by the custodian of a business record of

regularly conducted activity or another qualified person that, if falsely made, would subject the maker to criminal penalty under the laws of the state of Louisiana.

(3) "Business" includes a business, institution, association, profession, occupation, and calling of every kind, whether or not conducted for profit.

Acts 2008, No. 178, §1.

Art. 804. Hearsay exceptions; declarant unavailable

A. Definition of unavailability. Except as otherwise provided by this Code, a declarant is "unavailable as a witness" when the declarant cannot or will not appear in court and testify to the substance of his statement made outside of court. This includes situations in which the declarant:

(1) Is exempted by ruling of the court on the ground of privilege from testifying concerning the subject matter of his statement;

(2) Persists in refusing to testify concerning the subject matter of his statement despite an order of the court to do so;

(3) Testifies to a lack of memory of the subject matter of his statement;

(4) Is unable to be present or to testify at the hearing because of death or then existing physical or mental illness, infirmity, or other sufficient cause; or

(5) Is absent from the hearing and the proponent of his statement has been unable to procure his attendance by process or other reasonable means. A declarant is not unavailable as a witness if his exemption, refusal, claim of lack of memory, inability, or absence is due to the procurement or wrong-doing of the proponent of his statement for the purpose of preventing the witness from attending or testifying.

B. Hearsay exceptions. The following are not excluded by the hearsay rule if the declarant is unavailable as a witness:

(1) Former testimony. Testimony given as a witness at another hearing of the same or a different proceeding, if the party against whom the testimony is now offered, or, in a civil action or proceeding, a party with a similar interest, had an opportunity and similar motive to develop the testimony by direct, cross, or redirect examination. Testimony given in another proceeding by an expert witness in the form of opinions or inferences, however, is not admissible under this exception.

(2) Statement under belief of impending death. A statement made by a declarant while believing that his death was imminent, concerning the cause or circumstances of what he believed to be his impending death.

(3) Statement against interest. A statement which was at the time of its making so far contrary to the declarant's pecuniary or proprietary interest, or so far tended to subject him to civil or criminal liability, or to render invalid a claim by him against another, that a reasonable man in his position would not have made the statement unless he believed it to be true. A statement tending to expose the declarant to criminal liability and offered to exculpate the accused is not admissible unless corroborating circumstances clearly indicate the trustworthiness of the statement.

(4) Statement of personal or family history. (a) A statement, made before the controversy, concerning the declarant's own birth, adoption, marriage, divorce, filiation, relationship by blood, adoption, or marriage, ancestry, or other similar fact of personal or family history, even though declarant had no means of acquiring personal knowledge of the matter stated; or

(b) A statement, made before the controversy, concerning the foregoing matters, and death also, of another person, if the declarant was related to the other by blood, adoption, or marriage or was so intimately associated with the other's family as to be likely to have accurate information concerning the matter declared.

(5) Complaint of sexually assaultive behavior. A statement made by a person under the age of twelve years and the statement is one of initial or otherwise trustworthy complaint of sexually assaultive behavior.

(6) Other exceptions. In a civil case, a statement not specifically covered by any of the foregoing exceptions if the court determines that considering all pertinent circumstances in the particular case the statement is trustworthy, and the proponent of the evidence has adduced or made a reasonable effort to adduce all other admissible evidence to establish the fact to which the proffered statement relates and the proponent of the statement makes known in writing to the adverse party and to the court his intention to offer the statement and the particulars of it, including the name and address of the declarant, sufficiently in advance of the trial or hearing to provide the adverse party with a fair opportunity to prepare to meet it. If, under the circumstances of a particular case, giving of this notice was not practicable or failure to give notice is found by the court to have been excusable, the court may authorize a delayed notice to be given, and in that event the opposing party is entitled to a recess, continuance, or other appropriate relief sufficient to enable him to prepare to meet the evidence.

(7)(a) Forfeiture by wrongdoing. A statement offered against a party that has engaged or acquiesced in wrongdoing that was intended to, and did, procure the unavailability of the declarant as a witness.

(b) A party seeking to introduce statements under the forfeiture by wrongdoing hearsay exception shall establish, by a preponderance of the evidence, that the party against whom the statement is offered, engaged or acquiesced in the wrongdoing.

Acts 1988, No. 515, §1, eff. Jan. 1, 1989; Acts 1995, No. 346, §1; Acts 1995, No. 1300, §§1 and 2; Acts 1997, No. 577, §§2, 4; Acts 2004, No. 26, §4; Acts 2009, No. 7, §1; Acts 2010, No. 543, §1.

Art. 805. Hearsay within hearsay

Hearsay included within hearsay is not excluded under the hearsay rule if each part of the combined statements conforms with an exception to the hearsay rule provided by legislation.

Acts 1988, No. 515, §1, eff. Jan. 1, 1989.

Art. 806. Attacking and supporting credibility of declarant

When a hearsay statement, or a statement defined in Article 801(D)(2)(c) or (D)(3), has been admitted in evidence, the credibility of the declarant may be attacked, and if attacked may be supported, by any evidence which would be admissible for those purposes if declarant had testified as a witness. Evidence of a statement or conduct by the declarant at any time, offered to attack the declarant's credibility, is not subject to any requirement that he may have been afforded an opportunity to deny or explain. If the party against whom a hearsay statement has been admitted calls the declarant as a witness, the party is entitled to examine him on the statement as a witness identified with an adverse party.

Acts 1988, No. 515, §1, eff. Jan. 1, 1989.

CHAPTER 9. AUTHENTICATION AND IDENTIFICATION

Art. 901. Requirement of authentication or identification

A. General provision. The requirement of authentication or identification as a condition precedent to admissibility is satisfied by evidence sufficient to support a finding that the matter in question is what its proponent claims.

B. Illustrations. By way of illustration only, and not by way of limitation, the following are examples of authentication or identification conforming with the requirements of this Article:

(1) Testimony of witness with knowledge. Testimony that a matter is what it is claimed to be.

(2) Nonexpert opinion on handwriting. Nonexpert opinion as to the genuineness of handwriting, based upon familiarity not acquired for purposes of the litigation.

(3) Comparison by trier or expert witness. Comparison by the trier of fact or by expert witnesses with specimens which have been authenticated.

(4) Distinctive characteristics and the like. Appearance, contents, substance, internal patterns, or other distinctive characteristics, taken in conjunction with circumstances.

(5) Voice identification. Identification of a voice, whether heard firsthand or through mechanical or electronic transmission or recording, by opinion based upon hearing the voice at any time under circumstances connecting it with the alleged speaker.

(6) Telephone conversations. Telephone conversations, by evidence that a call was made to the number assigned at the time by the telephone company to a particular person or business, if:

(a) In the case of a person, circumstances, including self-identification, show the person answering to be the one called; or

(b) In the case of a business, the call was made to a place of business and the conversation related to business reasonably transacted over the telephone.

(7) Public records or reports. Evidence that a writing authorized by law to be recorded or filed and in fact recorded or filed in a public office, or a purported public record, report, statement, or data compilation, in any form, is from the public office where items of this nature are kept.

(8) Ancient documents or data compilation. Evidence that a document or data compilation, in any form:

(a) Is in such condition as to create no suspicion concerning its authenticity;

(b) Was in a place where it, if authentic, would likely be; and

(c) Has been in existence thirty years or more at the time it is offered.

(9) Process or system. Evidence describing a process or system used to produce a result and showing that the process or system produces an accurate result.

(10) Methods provided by legislation. Any method of authentication or identification provided by Act of Congress or by Act of the Louisiana Legislature.

Acts 1988, No. 515, §1, eff. Jan. 1, 1989.

Art. 902. Self-authentication

Extrinsic evidence of authenticity as a condition precedent to admissibility is not required with respect to the following:

(1) Domestic public documents under seal. A document bearing a seal, including electronically generated documents logically associated with electronically generated seals, purporting to be that of the United States, or of any state, district, commonwealth, territory, or insular possession thereof, or the Panama Canal Zone, or the Trust Territory of the Pacific Islands, or of a political subdivision, department, officer, or agency thereof, and a signature purporting to be an attestation or execution.

(2) Domestic public documents not under seal. (a) Domestic public documents generally. A document purporting to bear the signature in his official capacity of an officer or employee of any entity included in Paragraph (1) hereof, having no seal, if a public officer having a seal and having official duties in the district or political subdivision of the officer or employee certifies under seal that the signer has the official capacity and that the signature is genuine.

(b) Certified Louisiana public documents. A purported record, book, paper, or other document of the State of Louisiana, or of a department, board, or agency thereof or of a political subdivision of the state or a department, board, or agency of such a subdivision when certified as being the original by an officer or employee who identifies his official position and who either has custody of the document or who is otherwise authorized to make such a certification.

(3) Foreign public documents. A document purporting to be executed or attested in his official capacity by a person authorized by the laws of a foreign country to make the execution or attestation, and accompanied by a final certification as to the genuineness of the signature and official position (a) of the executing or attesting person, or (b) of any foreign official whose certificate of genuineness of signature and official position relates to the execution or attestation or is in a chain of certificates of genuineness of signature and official position relating to the execution or attestation. A final certification may be made by a secretary of embassy or legation, consul general, consul, vice consul, or consular agent of the United States, or a diplomatic or consular official of the foreign country assigned or accredited to the United States. If reasonable opportunity has been given to all parties to investigate the authenticity and accuracy of official documents, the court may, for good cause shown, order that they be treated as presumptively authentic without final certification or permit them to be evidenced by an attested summary with or without final certification.

(4) Presumptions under Acts of Congress and the Louisiana Legislature. Any signature, document, or other matter declared by Act of Congress or by Act of the Louisiana Legislature to be presumptively or prima facie genuine or authentic.

(5) Official publications. Books, pamphlets, or other publications purporting to be issued by public authority.

(6) Newspapers and periodicals. Printed materials purporting to be newspapers or periodicals.

(7) Trade inscriptions and the like. Inscriptions, signs, tags, or labels purporting to have been affixed in the course of business and indicating ownership, control, or origin.

(8) Authentic acts, acknowledged acts, and other instruments attested by witnesses. (a) Authentic acts, acts under private signature duly acknowledged, and instruments attested by witnesses and accompanied by affidavits, as provided by Louisiana law, whether executed in Louisiana or elsewhere. (b) Documents executed in a jurisdiction other than Louisiana accompanied by a certificate of acknowledgment executed in the manner provided by the laws of that jurisdiction by a notary public or other officer authorized by law to take acknowledgments.

(9) Commercial paper and related documents. Commercial paper, signatures thereon, and documents relating thereto to the extent provided by general commercial law.

(10) Labor reports. A copy of a report from the Louisiana Workforce Commission, or from any state or federal reporting agency, which is in the possession of a field officer of the support enforcement services program, office of children and family, Department of Children and Family Services, introduced as evidence in any child or spousal support proceeding. "Field officer" means any person designated or authorized as a field officer pursuant to the provisions of R.S. 46:236.1.8.

(11) Certified records of a regularly conducted business activity in criminal cases. In criminal cases, the original or a copy of a record of a regularly conducted business activity that meets the requirements of Article 803(6), as shown by a certification of the custodian or another qualified person, and that complies with Louisiana law, including R.S. 13:3733 through 3733.2, or a rule prescribed by the Louisiana Supreme Court. Before the trial or hearing, the proponent shall give an adverse party reasonable written notice of the intent to offer the record and shall make the record and certification available for inspection so that the party has a fair opportunity to challenge it.

Acts 1988, No. 515, §1, eff. Jan. 1, 1989; Acts 1997, No. 604, §1; Acts 2008, No. 743, §7, eff. July 1, 2008; Acts 2010, No. 238, §5; Acts 2010, No. 541, §1; Acts 2017, No. 409, §1.

Art. 903. Subscribing witness' testimony unnecessary

The testimony of a subscribing witness is not necessary to authenticate a writing unless required by the laws of the jurisdiction whose laws govern the validity of the writing.

Acts 1988, No. 515, §1, eff. Jan. 1, 1989.

Art. 904. Self-authentication of copies of public documents

When an original public document is deemed authentic without proof by extrinsic evidence as provided in Article 902(1), (2), or (3), a purported copy of the document also shall be deemed authentic when certified as true or correct by the custodian or other person authorized to make that certification, by certificate complying with Article 902(1), (2), or (3).

Acts 1988, No. 515, §1, eff. Jan. 1, 1989.

Art. 905. Self-authentication of other public records

A. Self-authentication. Extrinsic evidence of authenticity as a condition precedent to admissibility is not required with respect to a document purporting to be a document authorized by law to be recorded or filed and actually recorded or filed in a public office, including data compilations in any form, when it is certified as being true or correct by the custodian or other person authorized to make the certification, by certificate complying with Article 902(1), (2), or (3) and when, by statute, it is made to be presumptively or prima facie genuine or authentic.

B. Copy of original document described in Paragraph A. A document which purports to be a copy of an original document described in Paragraph A shall be deemed as authentic as the original when certified as true or correct by the custodian or other person authorized to make the certification, by certificate complying with Article 902(1), (2), or (3).

C. Copy of other public records. A document which purports to be a copy of an original document, other than a document described in Paragraph A, which is recorded or filed in a public office, including a data compilation in any form, shall be prima facie evidence that the copy accurately reflects the contents of the document which is filed or recorded when the copy is certified as true or correct by the custodian or other person authorized to make the certification, by certificate complying with Article 902(1), (2), or (3).

Acts 1988, No. 515, §1, eff. Jan. 1, 1989.

CHAPTER 10. CONTENTS OF WRITINGS,

RECORDINGS, AND PHOTOGRAPHS

Art. 1001. Definitions

For purposes of this Chapter the following definitions are applicable:

(1) Writings and recordings. "Writings" and "recordings" consist of letters, words, numbers, sounds, or their equivalent, set down by handwriting, typewriting, printing, photostating, photographing, magnetic impulse, mechanical or electronic recording, or other form of data compilation.

(2) Photographs. "Photographs" include still photographs, X-ray films, video tapes, motion pictures, and their equivalents.

(3) Original. An "original" of a writing or recording is the writing or recording itself or any counterpart intended to have the same effect by a person executing or issuing it. An "original" of a photograph includes the negative or any print therefrom. If data are stored in or copied onto a computer or similar device, including any portable or hand-held computer or electronic storage device, any printout or other output readable by sight, shown to reflect the data accurately, is an "original".

(4) Optical disk imaging system. An "optical disk imaging system" is a storage system that utilizes non-erasable Write Once Read Many (WORM) optical storage technology to record information on an optical disk with the use of laser technology, and that utilizes laser technology to retrieve and read previously stored information.

(5) Duplicate. A "duplicate" is a counterpart produced by the same impression as the original, or from the same matrix, or by means of photography, including enlargements and miniatures, or by mechanical or electronic re-recording, or electronic imaging, or by chemical reproduction, or by an optical disk imaging system, or by other equivalent techniques, which accurately reproduces the original.

(6) Electronic imaging. "Electronic imaging" is the process of storing and retrieving any record, document, data, or other information through the use of electronic data processing, or computerized, digital, or optical scanning, or other electronic imaging system.
Acts 1988, No. 515, §1, eff. Jan. 1, 1989; Acts 1995, No. 346, §1; Acts 2001, No. 941, §1; Acts 2003, No. 1135, §1, eff. July 2, 2003.

Art. 1002. Requirement of original

To prove the content of a writing, recording, or photograph, the original writing, recording, or photograph is required, except as otherwise provided by this Code or other legislation.
Acts 1988, No. 515, §1, eff. Jan. 1, 1989.

Art. 1003. Admissibility of duplicates

A duplicate is admissible to the same extent as an original unless:

(1) A genuine question is raised as to the authenticity of the original;

(2) In the circumstances it would be unfair to admit the duplicate in lieu of the original; or

(3) The original is a testament offered for probate, a contract on which the claim or defense is based, or is otherwise closely related to a controlling issue.
Acts 1988, No. 515, §1, eff. Jan. 1, 1989; Acts 2001, No. 941, §1; Acts 2003, No. 1135, §1, eff. July 1, 2003.

Art. 1003.1. Electronic duplicates

A duplicate may not be deemed inadmissible or excluded from evidence solely because it is in electronic form or is a reproduction of electronically imaged or stored records, documents, data, or other information.
Acts 2001, No. 941, §1.

Art. 1004. Admissibility of other evidence of contents

The original is not required, and other evidence of the contents of a writing, recording, or photograph is admissible if:

(1) Originals lost or destroyed. All originals are lost or have been destroyed, unless the proponent lost or destroyed them in bad faith;

(2) Original not obtainable. No original can be obtained by any available judicial process or procedure;

(3) Original in possession of opponent. At a time when an original was under the control of the party against whom offered, he was put on notice, by the pleadings or otherwise, that the contents would be a subject of proof at the hearing, and he does not produce the original at the hearing;

(4) Collateral matters. The writing, recording, or photograph is not closely related to a controlling issue; or

(5) Impracticality of producing original. The original, because of its location, permanent fixture, or otherwise, cannot as a practical matter be produced in court; or the cost or other consideration to be incurred in securing the original is prohibitive and it appears that a copy will serve the evidentiary purpose.
Acts 1988, No. 515, §1, eff. Jan. 1, 1989.

Art. 1005. Public records

The contents of an official record, or of a document authorized to be recorded or filed and actually recorded or filed, including data compilations in any form, if otherwise admissible, may be proved by copy, certified as correct in accordance with Article 902 or testified to be correct by a witness who has compared it with the original. If a copy which complies with the foregoing cannot be obtained by the exercise of reasonable diligence, then other evidence of the contents may be given.
Acts 1988, No. 515, §1, eff. Jan. 1, 1989.

Art. 1006. Summaries

The contents of otherwise admissible voluminous writings, recordings, or photographs which cannot conveniently be examined in court may be presented in the form of a chart, summary,

or calculation. The originals, or duplicates, shall be made available for examination or copying, or both, by other parties at a reasonable time and place. The court may order that they be produced in court.
Acts 1988, No. 515, §1, eff. Jan. 1, 1989.

Art. 1007. Testimony or written admission of party

Contents of writings, recordings, or photographs may be proved by the testimony or, in a civil case, deposition of the party against whom offered or by his written admission, without accounting for the nonproduction of the original.
Acts 1988, No. 515, §1, eff. Jan. 1, 1989.

Art. 1008. Functions of court and jury

When the admissibility of other evidence of contents of writings, recordings, or photographs under these articles depends upon the fulfillment of a condition of fact, the question whether the condition has been fulfilled is ordinarily for the court to determine in accordance with the provisions of Article 104. However, when an issue is raised (1) whether the asserted writing ever existed, or (2) whether another writing, recording, or photograph produced at the trial is the original, or (3) whether other evidence of contents correctly reflects the contents, the issue is for the trier of fact to determine as in the case of other issues of fact.
Acts 1988, No. 515, §1, eff. Jan. 1, 1989.

CHAPTER 11. MISCELLANEOUS RULES

Art. 1101. Applicability

A. Proceedings generally; rule of privilege.

(1) Except as otherwise provided by legislation, the provisions of this Code shall be applicable to the determination of questions of fact in all contradictory judicial proceedings and in proceedings to confirm a default judgment. Juvenile adjudication hearings in delinquency proceedings shall be governed by the provisions of this Code applicable to civil cases. Juvenile adjudication hearings in delinquency proceedings shall be governed by the provisions of this Code applicable to criminal cases.

(2) Furthermore, except as otherwise provided by legislation, Chapter 5 of this Code with respect to testimonial privileges applies to all stages of all actions, cases, and proceedings where there is power to subpoena witnesses, including administrative, juvenile, legislative, military courts-martial, grand jury, arbitration, medical review panel, and judicial proceedings, and the proceedings enumerated in Paragraphs B and C of this Article.

B. Limited applicability. Except as otherwise provided by Article 1101(A)(2) and other legislation, in the following proceedings, the principles underlying this Code shall serve as guides to the admissibility of evidence. The specific exclusionary rules and other provisions, however, shall be applied only to the extent that they tend to promote the purposes of the proceeding.

(1) Worker's compensation cases.

(2) Child custody cases.

(3) Revocation of probation hearings.

(4) Preliminary examinations in criminal cases, and the court may consider evidence that would otherwise be barred by the hearsay rule.

(5) All proceedings before mayors' courts and justice of the peace courts.

(6) Peace bond hearings.

(7) Extradition hearings.

(8) Hearings on motions and other summary proceedings involving questions of fact not dispositive of or central to the disposition of the case on the merits, or to the dismissal of the case, excluding in criminal cases hearings on motions to suppress evidence and hearings to determine mental capacity to proceed.

C. Rules inapplicable. Except as otherwise provided by Article 1101(A)(2) and other legislation, the provisions of this Code shall not apply to the following:

(1) The determination of questions of fact preliminary to admissibility of evidence when the issue is to be determined by the court under Article 104.

(2) Proceedings with respect to release on bail.

(3) Disposition hearings in juvenile cases.

(4) Sentencing hearings except as provided in Code of Criminal Procedure Article 905.2 in capital cases.

(5) Small claims court proceedings except as provided in R.S. 13:5203 and 13:5207.

(6) Proceedings before grand juries except as provided by Code of Criminal Procedure Article 442.

D. Discretionary applicability. Notwithstanding the limitations on the applicability of this Code stated in Paragraphs A, B, and C of this Article, in all judicial proceedings a court may rely upon the provisions of this Code with respect to judicial notice, authentication and identification, and proof of contents of writings, recordings, and photographs as a basis for admitting evidence or making a finding of fact.

Acts 1988, No. 515, §1, eff. Jan. 1, 1989; Acts 1988, 2nd Ex. Sess. No. 7, §1, eff. Jan. 1, 1989; Acts 1992, No. 376, §3, eff. Jan. 1, 1993.

{{NOTE: SECTION 12 OF ACTS 1988, NO. 515, PROVIDES AS FOLLOWS:

Section 12.(1) The provisions of this Act shall govern and regulate all civil proceedings commenced and criminal prosecutions instituted on or after the effective date of this Act.

(2) Furthermore, it shall govern and regulate all hearings, trials or retrials, and other proceedings to which it is applicable which are commenced on or after the effective date of this Act, except to the extent that its application in a particular action pending when the Act takes effect would not be feasible or would work injustice, in which event former evidentiary rules apply.

(3) All of the provisions of this Act shall become effective on January 1, 1989.}}

Art. 1102. Title

This Code may be known and cited as the "Louisiana Code of Evidence."

Acts 1988, No. 515, §1, eff. Jan. 1, 1989.

Art. 1103. Repealed by Acts 1995, No. 1300, §2

Art. 1104. State v. Prieur; pretrial; burden of proof

The burden of proof in a pretrial hearing held in accordance with State v. Prieur, 277 So.2d 126 (La. 1973), shall be identical to the burden of proof required by Federal Rules of Evidence Article IV, Rule 404.

Acts 1994, 3rd Ex. Sess., No. 51, §2.